LIVING WITH
MULTIPLE
SCLEROSIS

LIVING WITH
MULTIPLE
SCLEROSIS

The Ripple Effect

NANCY WAYLAND

LIVING WITH MULTIPLE SCLEROSIS
THE RIPPLE EFFECT

iUniverse books may be ordered through booksellers or by contacting:

iUniverse
1663 Liberty Drive
Bloomington, IN 47403
www.iuniverse.com
1-800-Authors (1-800-288-4677)

ISBN: 978-1-5320-2718-5 (sc)
ISBN: 978-1-5320-2719-2 (e)

Library of Congress Control Number: 2017910142

Print information available on the last page.

iUniverse rev. date: 07/03/2017

Contents

FOREWORD

This is my life's story. I didn't choose to write this book because my life has always been great, but because I've learned so much about myself as I've journeyed through these past 53 years, and I have been encouraged by numerous people to share my story. Not because my journey has been revolutionizing, or miraculous even, but because not any one of us is guaranteed a perfect life. We aren't even guaranteed a tomorrow. If we are lucky enough to wake up each morning, we are given what we have on a daily basis and it is how we take the moments that shape our lives, as well as the lives of the people around us. Everything that we do or is done to us, affects the people around us in some way. My husband came up with the concept of The Ripple Effect while I was writing this book, I think in part because he has seen as well as known the ripple effect and has witnessed the many ways the ripples MS creates in our lives as well as our loved ones.

I give God all the credit for everything wonderful that has happened in my life, and yes, even the not-so wonderful things. I am a firm believer that everything happens for a reason, and that someday we each will discover all the reasons behind our particular circumstances, when we are welcomed into the gates of heaven by our maker. Of course, I know that I wish to know the meanings behind my situations *before* that time, and that is where faith and prayer come in. At least that is what has kept my mind and heart content until I reach that point at the end of my life… and I am in no rush to reach that point!

DEDICATION

I dedicate this book to my husband, Steve, without whose encouragement throughout the writing of the book, I might never have completed this dream of mine to be a published author. My parents, Virles and Barbara Wasson, have supported me throughout life in whatever crazy ideas I happened to pursue. My children, Hunter Austin and Lily Sloan, who continue to express their love and support to me. I know I haven't always been a perfect mother, but thanks for helping me learn and grow as a parent throughout your growing years. My sisters; Jacque Hill and Carol Morgan, for being excellent role models for their baby sister, and their spouses Glen and Allen. My six nieces and nephews, and every one of my great-nieces and nephews, thank you for being a part of my life, I love each one of you more than you will ever know.

I also want to thank my in-laws, Dr. Jan Wayland and Rev. John Barton, and Drs. Bob and Jane Wayland for always being supportive to both Steve and me through difficult times. Last but certainly not least, I also wish to thank Steve's brothers; Bill & Terry Wayland, and their wives Kathy & Pauline, and Ryan Hardy, as well as their children for being a great means of moral support and social inspiration in our lives. I am blessed to have so many wonderful people as part of my family!

I would like to add a very special thanks to my nephew, John Wasson Morgan for his work in designing the cover photo for my book. jwmphotography.com

DISCLAIMER

I would like to thank the real-life members of my family and friends portrayed in this book for allowing me to record my memories of life as I recalled them. I recognize that their memories of the events described in this book are different than my own. They are each fine, decent, and hard-working people. The book was not intended to hurt them in any way. I regret any unintentional harm resulting from the publishing and marketing of The Ripple Effect: My Life with Multiple Sclerosis.

My Growing Years

My childhood was not idyllic by any means, but it sure seems that way when it is compared to today's society. I was born to my parents in late December of the year 1963, which makes me very literally one of the last children to be born into the Baby Boom generation. My birth completed the family of five that consisted of my parents, my two older sisters, and me.

We lived in Arkadelphia, AR, or rather, 11 miles outside of Arkadelphia. Those eleven miles meant the difference between a local telephone number with a prefix of 246, and a long-distance phone number, a 366 prefix, from town. It also meant the difference between paved streets and gravel roads, city services such as water and electricity, and well water. Another important difference is electricity that stays on during a thunderstorm, versus electricity that gets disrupted at the first hint of a thunderstorm. Neighborhood blocks versus communities, stop signs at every corner, versus cows in almost every pasture. It was a rural upbringing, and is a main reason that my husband and I choose to live in the same area, but I'm getting ahead of myself.

My sisters and I lived a very "Beaver Cleaver" type of life. Dinner was always around the dinner table, bicycles were (almost) always parked on the carport, and each meal began with bowed heads and a prayer.

My parents owned their own company, with my mom's father. It is a business that cuts timber from property, then sells the wood to companies such as International Paper or Georgia Pacific. Basically, my mom ran the office which included contracts with the property owners and the timber buyers, as well as payroll for each individual hauler. It was her duty to receive each week's order for the type of wood and the amount. My father and grandfather dealt with the property owners and managed all the teams of haulers. These men would then receive their orders, cut the required trees, and haul them on pulpwood trucks to the woodyard where each load of timber was weighed before the team received their next assignment.

These men, (and at least one woman) were the hardest working people I have yet to see. They would be in the woods working, no matter the outside temperature, and most times even in the rain, as long as it wasn't too muddy to get the pulpwood trucks into the woods. It was imperative that each crew keep their own trucks in good working condition, so that they could make money to feed their families.

There would be slow times in the business, and times when it was too wet to take the trucks into the woods, or even maybe the wood orders from the companies that buy wood might be low that week. It all worked on a large supply and demand over-arching way, and if one step was not keeping up its share of the load, then a lot of people would be affected.

My parents and grandfather ran the business while always keeping the men, the haulers, in mind. Meanwhile, we lived comfortably. We were not rich, in any way. Neither my sisters nor I were ever denied clothes, gas for our cars, or money for school activities.

My oldest sister, Jacque, was the most social of the three of us, and she was a cheerleader throughout both high school and college. She had many friends, and never seemed to be left on a weekend with nothing to do. Carol is the pretty sister, or as Jacque and I call her, the *perfect* one. The blonde. Carol was always first in offering to help mom with chores *without complaining.* Jacque, mom, and I each have dark brown hair, but Carol has gotten my dad's light hair and most distressing to me of all, his dark skin tone. (I remain a little jealous of that.)

Dad and Carol always look so tan in the summers, while Jacque, mom, and I are so fair-skinned that we almost look translucent. Luckily, the advent of self-tanning lotions has virtually eliminated the translucent problem. To make matters worse, we were growing up in the '60's and '70's, the time of short shorts and tanned skin... skin cancer was not spoken about in the media until years later. No matter how hard I tried to get a golden glow to my skin, I would end up a bright pink, or worse, red!

I feel sorry for mom, because she raised three bona-fide daddy's girls. Mom could have used our help folding laundry, sweeping the kitchen, vacuuming the carpets, or endless other household chores, but we always seemed to find whatever our dad was doing at the time so much more interesting than chores. These things ranged from welding a trailer hitch to gluing whatever is broken back together, to working with the cows, to watching him train his bird dogs.

I know that I found watching Dad fix something in his shop behind the house much more engaging than housework. Of course, it didn't help that Dad was always outside. He has never been one to sit and watch sports on television on the weekends, for example. If there is daylight outside, he is outside working on something. I believe that his strong work ethic was ingrained in him from an early age.

Dad's family of seven lived in Southeast Arkansas, where they were sharecroppers. I have heard many stories of my grandmother taking my father to the cotton fields while he was in diapers, not even walking yet. Granny would sit dad at the end of a row of cotton, then go pick a row, leaving dad to fend for himself until her row was finished. It borders on child abuse now, but dad had three older sisters and an older brother whom I am sure would take turns watching him.

Dad's oldest sister had the first grandchild only ten years after my dad was born, and Dad and Butch practically grew up as brothers. In fact, I grew up thinking that Butch was my uncle, not my cousin. I still love to hear the stories of the ways Dad and Jimmy, his brother, helped to "raise" Butch. It's amazing to me that Butch even survived his childhood, much less even made it to adulthood. They taught Butch how to ride a bicycle, hunt, fish, drive, and get into all sorts of mischief over the years. Granny had an easygoing personality and heavy Pentecostal faith that enabled her to not sweat the small stuff, which I assumed enabled her to withstand the adolescent and teen years of raising the three boys. From what I've been told, they were each rebellious in their own ways.

With my dad's work ethic, and my mom's head for finances, it was no surprise that my sisters and I grew up with huge respect for our parents. Our parents worked hard, invested wisely, and spent frugally so that the three of us girls would have a nice home in the country and everything we could possibly want. We rarely took family vacations to any of the amusement parks and attractions that abound in our country, but we would spend weeks at a time camping in one of the state parks in our area.

Camping is still one of my favorite memories of summer, although I haven't camped in years. I guess being in wheelchair stops me from trying to camp. I'm sure there are handicapped-accessible camping sites available around the country, we have just not explored them yet. That is my next big goal: Go camping.

It may sound strange to read this, but one of my fondest memories is camping with my family at Blanchard Springs in northern Arkansas, and my sisters and I would pretend our watermelon was a dolphin! It may sound ridiculous to hear now, but the watermelon would be in the cool water's edge at our camp site, cooling in the shallow water for dad could cut it for us to enjoy. I don't recall which of the three of us began imagining that the slick, water-cooled melon resembled Flipper from a favorite television show, but to us the watermelon WAS Flipper!

We would sit on top of the enormous melon and

imagine that we were Flipper's caretakers and that we could swim the ocean with him until dark, or dinnertime, whichever came first. My husband and friends laugh whenever I mention the watermelon-Flipper story, and I guess I can understand why. I remember playing on the watermelon in the shallow water with my sisters fondly. Even today, a mention of our watermelon Flipper brings smiles to each of our faces.

Summers were spent at home for the most part, and it wasn't until I was older that I realized that my friends' families would spend their summers vacationing at various spots around the country. I never felt left out, until my friends would begin re-telling their families' vacation stories each fall in school. Although I may have been jealous of them because their families took summer vacations, I knew in my heart that it would be too difficult for my parents to step away from their business just to take a family vacation.

I said before that the company was a well-oiled machine that depended on all parts working together to turn a profit, and my parents always had their employees' livelihoods in the back of their minds. They didn't want any of the employees to suffer, missing weeks' worth of pay, because they realized that many of the men survived by barely scraping enough money to buy groceries on a weekly basis. This is not to say that we never took family vacations.

I recall visiting Williamsburg, Virginia one summer during my teen years, and we have the photos to prove just how sullen and miserable I was that summer. As I remember, I was a spoiled teenager, expecting the world to revolve around me. Why are teenagers so difficult? Why do they think that the world owes them something? I just wish that I could go back in time to shake some sense into that adolescent me!

We also rented a beach house in North Carolina in the late '70's. It was a small house, the back porch was uninhabitable during high tide each day, as the waves would pound whomever dared to sit on the porch watching the tide roll in. It is a peaceful existence to live on the beach, and I still remember falling asleep to the never-ending sound of waves crashing on the sand. Sound machines may have the same sounds for people to use while falling asleep, but unless you can feel a light ocean breeze across your cheek, it's just not the same.

I feel the same way about crickets at night. A machine may be able to duplicate the sound, but unless it also duplicates the feel and sound of a light breeze through the leaves, it just doesn't work for me. In fact, when my husband Steve was settling in with a midnight shift, my sister Carol gave him one of those sound machines to aid his sleep in the daytime. It made me laugh and think, what a city boy, using a machine to listen to noises that were just outside his window!

I graduated from high school with an honor's diploma and I was in the top ten percent of my graduating class. Most of my friends stayed in Arkadelphia for college. Arkadelphia is the home to two universities, Ouachita Baptist and Henderson State. My parents had both attended Henderson, where my dad played basketball. Upon his graduation, they married and my oldest sister came along, followed by my other sister two years later. I didn't complete the family until 1963.

Although both of my parents and oldest sister are Henderson alumni, I followed Carol's steps and enrolled at the University of Arkansas. I did attend Henderson for one year, but that was because I was so head over heels in love with my high school boyfriend. Dave and I began dating in high school. We continued dating even though we ended up attending different universities in two different states.

Dave was 6'3" muscular, with jet back hair and piercing green eyes. Dave was not only a talented football player, he also had the brains behind his brawn. For those two reasons alone he was one of the most heavily recruited high school players in the state. He was even highly recruited nationwide, by schools such as Penn State, Notre Dame, UCLA, USC, Alabama, and all the teams in the Southwest Conference. Most of the top twenty schools leaned on him and his dad to allow their schools to become his college home. In the end, he had narrowed his choices to two schools, University of Arkansas and Southern Methodist University in Dallas. I naively assumed he would ultimately choose Arkansas, because that is where I planned to study. Naïve, that was me.

THE COLLEGE DECISION

One night as we sat on the floor in his den, Dave placed his arm around my shoulders in a very comforting way and he quietly told me that he had made his decision,

"Nancy, I've decided to go to SMU.". The words fell to the ground as if they were a dead weight. A hundred questions raced through my mind. I was heartbroken.

I finally found my voice, and asked him, "Why?" I couldn't trust my voice to say anything more.

He attempted to answer my question with what I assumed were platitudes given to him by the recruiters, as well as his father.

"I think Dallas offers me more opportunity for a successful future in business than Fayetteville would." It sounded like a stock answer to me. An answer he would give his high school teachers or coaches, not something he should be a saying to *me!*

At this time, I was planning to transfer my college credits to the University of Arkansas, where I had assumed he would be going to school, also. I had fantasized about walking to classes with him, hanging onto his arm as we explored Fayetteville and the surrounding areas, travelling back to Arkadelphia on non-game weekends, etc.

Dave's announcement took me by surprise, and I ran out of his house and down the street, hoping I had misunderstood him. My intentions were to go to a friend's house to seek solace and comfort, but I realized at the last minute that my friend must be at work, so I stood outside, pacing the street in front of Dave's house. I didn't want to go back into Dave's house at the time, but I needed to hear his reasoning behind this decision. I heard his front door open and close, so I knew he must be outside looking for me.

He walked up behind me, and without a sound, he hugged me close to his chest until my sobs subsided. I can now see that God was doing what is best for each of us, although I didn't understand it at the time. I realize now that God *always* knows what is best for us, although it took me twenty years to figure that one out.

I even entertained the idea of attending SMU for a few weeks, but ultimately kept my plans to transfer to the University of Arkansas in the Fall of 1983, and I am so glad that I did. Of course, I questioned myself at first. All my high school friends were firmly entrenched at their choices of universities by that time. I wanted to have more of an experience at a large school, several hours from home.

I didn't realize just how far Fayetteville was from Arkadelphia until my parents and sister, Carol had left me in my dorm room with a roommate I had not met until the day before on that autumn afternoon in 1983. Coming from such a small town to a college town whose student population was greater than the entire population of my hometown was quite a change.

Being alone at the University of Arkansas provided me with reasons to venture out and befriend other students at the school out of necessity. It was then that I realized how much I had let Dave's identity become my own. I had been living in his shadow for four years, and would have stayed firmly implanted there for the remainder of my college career had he chosen to come to the University of Arkansas.

We worked it out somehow; we each rang up enormous telephone bills, as well as kept the postal service in business with frequent letters. Yes, actual letters with stamps on them as there was no email, Facebook, Instagram, or Twitter at the time.

I made good friends while at the University of Arkansas. Looking back, I am *glad* Dave didn't choose to play football there. That would have tainted many of my fond memories of the university, and I'm afraid that would have ruined the memories of my college experience for me.

As it stands, I thoroughly enjoyed my years in Fayetteville, and am still in contact with the friends I made there. In my first year there, I made some good friends in the dorm and we chose to live off-campus for the following two and a half years it took me to complete my degree. I chose not to go through the sorority rush for new members in the fall. I don't know why I chose not to become a member of any of the fine sororities on campus, but through my roommates, I eventually became a Little Sister to one of the fraternities. As it happened, my

Big Brother married my roommate after graduation, the reality of the relationship was not nearly as incestuous as it sounds, and I was asked to sing in their wedding.

I planned to graduate in December 1985. It was bittersweet leaving campus for my hometown that last time. I was finished with school, but didn't exactly know what my plans were for after the Christmas break. I not only said goodbye to my roommates and friends for the Christmas holiday, but for real. I wouldn't be returning in January with everyone else for another semester. That fact should have made me ecstatic, instead I shed tears all the way down Boston Mountain, leaving the beautiful Ozarks in my rearview mirror. Once home, I settled into my old bedroom and proceeded trying to find a job.

GETTING THE FIRST JOB:
STILL WATERS

I had sent my resume into a business that advertised in the *Dallas Morning News* on a Saturday during football season, when I was in town for one of SMU's football games. I had received a call from the head of HR while packing to leave Fayetteville. As it just so happened, the head of HR was the sister of a childhood friend. After talking on the telephone a bit, she told me to give her a call whenever I was in Dallas next.

I did, a few weeks later, and she set up an interview with the large insurance company where she worked. We knew many of the same people, so it was more of a girlfriend's chat over coffee than an interview. I was called back for another interview three weeks later. I repeated the process once again, and at the end of this interview, was told the position of Account Representative was mine, I would finally reside in the same town as Dave and couldn't wait to begin "painting the town red" with Dave.

After my move to Dallas, I did enjoy being in a large city that offered so many events and attractions. Dave and I saw *Cirque du Solei,* Bruce Springfield, John Cougar Mellencamp, Huey Lewis and the News, the travelling company of the Broadway show *Cats,* and many other performances that Dallas has to offer, such as AC/DC, Guns n' Roses, and Metallica. We especially enjoyed going to see upcoming comedians at the various venues in town. Of course, I must mention the sports teams in Dallas: The Cowboys, The Rangers, and The Mavericks. Dave was an athlete and there weren't many home games that we missed, thanks to complementary tickets from contacts through my job.

I settled into my new job as an account representative at the state's largest personal and commercial insurance company. My duties included being responsible for several districts of the state, providing the salesmen and women with competitive quotes for each policy that was up for renewal, and making trips to each district office every quarter or so, depending on the number of renewals that I managed to help them retain. It was a young office, and the other account reps and I all got along great with one another. We were all within a few years difference in ages, single, and enjoyed the same kinds of entertainment when not at work. I was the newest and youngest of the group, but we all got along very well. That was a bonus for me. I automatically surrounded myself with some people I considered to be good friends, and they didn't disappoint.

The other Account Representatives and I became fast friends. Our backgrounds were as diverse as each individual. It was a fun office smack-dab in the center of downtown Dallas, where our company had our own twelve-story building across from City Hall. I was a part of the company called, generically enough, National General Agency. It is the part of the company that dealt with high-risk policies with premiums in the hundreds of thousands of dollars. I learned the ins and outs of the commercial property insurance quickly. I enjoyed travelling to "my" district offices because it was always nice to take a break from the office and the constant barrage of paper work that was constantly finding its way to my desk.

The job called for a lot of telephone work each day. Not only was I on the phone daily with each of the salesmen and women in my districts, but I was constantly playing telephone tag with the dozens of underwriters at some very large international insurance companies. Lloyd's of London was one of the companies with which I dealt on a regular basis, as well as companies in in New York, Los Angeles, and San Francisco. It was my job to shop each policy around to the different companies to get the best coverage/rate for our insureds. It was hectic, but always rewarding.

I was elated, I had a terrific first job, and I was at last in the same city as Dave. I couldn't wait! Our future as a Dallas couple, painting the town red, awaited us. By this time, marriage was the topic of conversation between us more often than not. A few months later, on our 9th anniversary of dating, he surprised me by dropping an engagement ring into my Champaign glass and asking me to marry him, right in the middle of the restaurant at the top of Reunion Tower. I was ecstatic, and of course I said yes. The applause rings in my head to this day. I had never been happier. The bright lights of Dallas seemed to shine even more brightly as we looked out the majestic windows to the city spread before us.

We decided to tell my family the following weekend, but unfortunately that weekend never came. The football team had a free weekend, (a weekend with no football game) so we planned a trip to our hometown to tell my family and his father. I knew that my parents would be happy for us. His father, on the other hand, I knew would be disappointed in his son. In his father's eyes, I was not good enough for his son. Not pretty enough. His father never really told me so, but I always felt his burning gaze of disapproval on me whenever we happened to be in the same vicinity.

As it turned out, I was alone in making those plans, I just didn't know I was making these plans for just one of us. By mid-week, when I hadn't seen Dave since the night of the engagement, I decided to surprise him while he was at his apartment studying. I was giddy with excitement as I turned my key in the lock. As soon as the door swung open I saw something that I never wanted or imagined seeing: my fiancée sitting on the couch with his arm around the waist of a perky, SMU coed with textbooks strewn on the floor. I was stunned, shocked, even as I stood frozen in place as if the air that had been in the room was noiselessly sucked out of the room. I don't even think I was breathing. Without even thinking about what I was doing, I slipped the beautiful engagement ring from my left hand and threw it, hard, and with a force I didn't know I had.

The ring landed beside Dave, but his eyes never met mine. He wouldn't even look at me, but I could tell from his guilty expression that the relationship between us was over. I turned and walked back to my car, miraculously holding back the tears until I was inside my apartment. After I had sobbed all the sobs I had within me, I took a deep breath, washed my face, and called home.

Yes, I called home. I wanted to talk to my mom. I needed to talk to her, to hear her tell me everything would be all right, even though it was months before I believed it myself. As it turned out, mom and dad had noticed Dave and me pulling away from one another in recent weeks. I didn't tell them about the ring or the wedding plans I was intending to make until much later. Dave and I never really said it was over, it was just understood between us that the past 9 years of our lives was behind us, as well as all the plans for our future together.

Mom said that she was afraid this would happen to our relationship. Two different universities, in two states, a tall, dark, and handsome football player (him), an attractive coed (me), cheerleaders and sorority girls at his school, fraternity brothers at mine. Dallas had all the trappings to lure Dave into the web of deceit that had become our normal lives: strip bars, Hooters, fraternities that would love to have a football player as a member, and most of all an alumni association whose members would do almost anything to help the team.

A case in point was the fact that I found out after the fact: Dave was arrested and taken to jail one night when he stole some DVDs at a local Hastings Music store. He tried to steal them, was caught, and put in jail. Who did he call? Not me! He called a SMU Alumni to bail him out of jail.

In fact, he didn't even tell me about the dumb-ass attempt to steal DVDs until over a month after the incident.

Of course, I forgave him. I still loved him at this point, and put my blinders securely in place and continued to live my life. A few weeks later came the proposal, which I now see as a feeble attempt to make up for his mistake, and to give me what he thought I wanted but was followed closely by the end of our relationship.

The remainder of 1986 was spent developing my friendships at work and church. I was fortunate to have a wide circle of friends, and we travelled around the state of Texas going to festivals of all kinds that summer. These friends were the people I worked with, as well as some of their friends. It was a fun group, and we all got along surprisingly well.

In the spring, the eight of us rented a condo in Breckenridge Colorado. We got along great; four guys and four girls. We were all single, none of us was dating another, and it was my group. Four of us worked together, others were college friends from Texas Christian University in Fort Worth, while another was the sister of one of the guys. We had great fun, even with the varying degrees of experience in snow skiing ranging from expert to a couple of beginners.

I had last skied in eighth grade when I had gone with a group from my hometown church. I was pleased to find that skiing was, to me at least, kind of like riding a bicycle. Once I had the skies strapped on, I was pleasantly surprised to find myself managing the intermediate courses rather well... as long as I continued to snow-plow!

I was in no way close to the expertise shown by my

talented friends, who were eagerly tackling the expert slopes over and over. The last day there, we decided as a group to tackle a black diamond slope together ... as a group! I was holding my own with the rest of the non-experts when suddenly it happened. I stood at the top, watching my friends make their way down the slope, my right leg feeling like a huge log of dead wood, unable to move. It felt as though my leg wasn't a part of my body at all.

I was unable to make it move, no matter how hard I tried. I stood, immobilized as my friends all made it to the bottom of the slope and other skiers were going around the statue that I had become. I could barely keep my balance on the packed snow. Each time another skier passed a little too closely to me, I felt my knees tremble. I just knew that I would soon be on my back, watching the other skiers pass me by. Eventually, I heard my name being called, and I turned my head to see who was calling my name.

"Nancy! What's wrong? Are you hurt?" It was Dana, inarguably the best skier of all of us. She had noticed that I hadn't followed the rest of the group down the slope, and thankfully had managed a ride from a member of the ski patrol to make her way to my side to see why I was imitating the Statue of Liberty.

"Hi Dana, I'm fine," I lied. "I think I'm just too tired to tackle this slope today. Besides, I must have twisted my knee getting off the lift..." I allowed my voice to trail as I was spewing lies as if it was normal for me to do so. The more I spoke, the more lies came out of my mouth and it was disturbing to me at how easily the words flowed off my tongue.

"Let me help you down the slope, it's late anyway, and let's meet up with the others and find someplace for dinner," Dana was always the one in our group who kept us on schedule.

I didn't tell her my leg was numb or that it felt like a chunk of wood. I was in denial. I didn't tell anyone about my leg, and while they all went to a popular bar & grill for dinner and drinks, I went back to the condo and fell asleep. I didn't even wake when they came back from dinner, tired, loud, and a little tipsy. The next morning my leg felt a little better, so I just limped a little to make sure they believed my knee story. I say it felt *a little* better, but it still wasn't feeling normal.

I couldn't quite put my finger on it, but I just knew my leg was feeling different. None of us wanted to leave, but we packed our suitcases rather begrudgingly and piled into the rented van for the trip to Denver to catch our flight back to Dallas and work. We were not nearly as jovial on the drive back to Denver, but we were all tired, and none of us was looking forward to getting back to work once we reached Dallas. However, each of us did return to work, somewhat begrudgingly. At least we had the memories of four fun-filled days on the slopes with good friends!

NOT THE DIAGNOSIS
I WAS EXPECTING

Sleep was not a problem that first night back in Dallas. I didn't even unpack my suitcase, only the necessities. I usually like to catch up on the newspapers after a trip out of town, but I could barely keep my eyes open long enough to wash my face and brush my teeth! I crawled into bed immediately following my nightly routine. I don't remember even dreaming that night, I just fell into a deep sleep.

The next morning begins as many mornings do, too early for my taste, with my alarm incessantly buzzing its obnoxious buzz. I force my eyes open, and stumble to the bathroom to splash water on my face. *Why am I so tired? I wonder, and then correct myself. I'm exhausted! But why? Did I hang out with my friends too late last night? No, that's not it, but it wouldn't be the first time I had dragged myself to work in downtown Dallas with a mild hangover. Maybe I was just exhausted from our ski trip.*

I told myself that everyone else probably felt the same way, and forced myself to drag my exhausted and yes, sore body to work. I eventually made it to work around 10:00, later that morning. I was supposed to be there at 8:00, but our boss would turn his head and pretend not to notice whenever any of us dragged in to work a little, or a lot, late. He was rather lenient with us in that way, as long as we got our work done and stayed on top of the high premium renewals. By 3:00, I was at my desk, talking on the phone to an agent in one of my assigned districts as my position often required, when Dan (the agent) asked me to write some information down for him.

I reached across my desk to pick up my pen, and I couldn't! I could not make my fingers grasp the pen! I laughed a little nervously, and told Dan my problem.

"I honestly can't even grab my pen, Dan. I don't know what's wrong, this has never happened to me before," I was speaking in a rather frightened tone. He dismissed the problem and told me to stop joking (I wasn't) and to get a quote for him on this policy ASAP! I managed to put the pen into my left hand and I proceeded to get the information I needed to get quotes from different companies, at various deductibles and price ranges. I was scribbling like a child, but I managed to get four quotes for Dan that day before leaving work.

I drove on Central Expressway to my apartment in a stupor. I was exhausted more than ever before, but somehow, I managed rush hour traffic in my half-awake state and I pulled into the parking lot at my apartment complex. It took several minutes to make my way to my door, but when I finally got the door open, I proceeded to go to my bedroom as quickly as I could, grabbing an apple from the table as I passed the dining room.

I collapsed on my bed as soon as I reached it, not even taking the time to change out of my work clothes. I lay on my back, staring at the ceiling, wondering what was happening to me. *Why was I so tired?* As I ate my apple, I watched the local news while reading the newspaper. I fell asleep before the weather came on, with only a few bites taken out of my apple.

The next thing I remember, the apartment was dark, and I had been sleeping for almost 7 hours! Was that really the correct time? The strange thing was that I still felt exhausted- not rested at all. I threw my apple away, changed my clothes, and you guessed it--fell asleep.

When I awoke at 8:20 a.m., my first inclination was to panic. *Work! What will I do about work?* I called my boss and told him that I had overslept, he wanted me to get into work as soon as I got dressed and made my way downtown. It was probably closer to 10:00 or even 10:30 before I made it to work. I was still so groggy, it felt as though I was showering, brushing my teeth, dressing in a fog, and yes, driving.

Every movement that I made was very slow and deliberate. I just attributed it to still being tired from the ski trip, or allergies to all of the grasses and trees that were blooming at the time. In fact, I could write almost every symptom off because of being tired from skiing or the allergy medicine I was taking.

When I finally made it to work, I chose to go in the back door of the office. That was a mistake. I had assumed the mailroom employees would be taking their morning break, but they weren't. In fact, little did I know, they had just been reprimanded by their supervisor for being tardy for work!

I received so many looks of disgust when I walked through the department; I knew something was going on. I began walking more quickly then and kept my eyes averted so as not to see all the scathing looks from my fellow employees. In this way, I avoided seeing the looks of disgust, but I certainly felt them! I then had to pass through two other departments, liability and personal insurances, and I received the same reaction from each member of those teams as well.

When I finally ducked into my office to slink behind my desk, Mr. Ross paged me to tell me to come to his office. I pushed myself out of my chair and begrudgingly made my way to his office. To my relief, he was concerned about me and just wanted to know what was going on in my life, why had I been coming in so late? Although I was unable to give him a reasonable answer, I said,

"Well, Mr. Ross, I really can't explain it, but I have just felt exhausted since our trip to Colorado. I really don't know what is wrong with me."

The truth was that I didn't have an answer for him, but I think he thought that I was staying out too late at night. Little did he know that the exact opposite was the truth- I had been sleeping almost non-stop since returning from Colorado.

"Just go home tonight and try to get plenty of rest. We'll see you here at eight o'clock tomorrow morning" he patted me on the back as I left his office.

"I'll be here bright and early tomorrow" I said as I

walked back to my office, fully intending to arrive at work by 7:30 the next day.

Before I left Mr. Ross's office, he encouraged me to see the company's RN at the clinic down the hall. She was a very nice lady, but she performed more the duties of a school nurse than a medical professional. Mrs. Matthews' duties included giving vaccinations, new employee physicals, taking temperatures and blood pressures. I sat in her office and recounted the story of the loss of control in my right hand. She asked if I had been doing anything out of the ordinary, so I mentioned that I had just returned from a ski trip. That was all she needed to hear,

"You must have injured your wrist in some way while you were skiing," she said. "And I imagine you didn't notice it because you were with friends, and having a good time. Just rest your wrist for the rest of the week, take some ibuprofen to keep the swelling down, and you'll be fine." I didn't tell her about my leg because quite frankly, I had put it at the back of my mind. I thanked her and made my way back to my office to finish my day.

Because I had come to work late again, I stayed late to finish up a few matters. When I finally made it back to my apartment, I was so tired that I repeated the events of the previous night and fell asleep with another apple in my left hand and my television blaring the news. I didn't even wake up until 7:00 the next morning. I was late again. What was more disturbing to me was the fact that my right hand and arm were both numb and tingling to my elbow. I called my mom to ask her what she thought I should do,

"Well Nancy, I really don't know. I think you just

injured it in some way while you were in Colorado. Why don't you call your great-aunt Christine and ask her for a referral to a physician? I'm sorry, honey, but let's just hope that it is nothing major. She gave my great-aunt's number, and said, "Call me when you get an appointment." Then she hung up the phone after we said our "I love you's". We both had to get to our respective offices. I did as she suggested, and the next day I had an appointment with my great-aunt's doctor.

I went to work late again, the third day in a row, but this time, I went directly to my boss's office. This time I held my head up and entered through the front door of the building.

Because of the numbness and weakness of my right hand and arm, I was carrying my work satchel, as well as my purse, in my left hand, which was causing me to walk a little bit lopsided. I paid no attention to that fact, because I was mainly consumed with the numbness in my right arm and hand. It wasn't "just" numbness that bothered me, but over the course of the morning the feeling in my hand and arm had changed somewhat.

If I thought about it, I could tell that it wasn't total numbness that was slowly overcoming my right side. My hand and arm were filled with tiny pin-pricks of pain, much like the feeling you get when your limb has fallen asleep and it is gradually getting the blood circulated again.

No matter what I did: shake my hand, clasp and unclasp my fingers, straighten my arm, bend my arm at the elbow, or *anything*, the pain would not go away. When a limb is regaining circulation after being cut off from the blood supply, the pain begins to lessen as the nerves, tendons, and muscles start receiving oxygenated blood. In my case, the pain continued to increase in intensity as the hours of the day wore on.

A little before lunch, I went to Mr. Ross' office to try to explain my behavior of the last few days, even though I couldn't explain it myself. He answered my knock to his door with his usual brusque "Come in."

I hesitated briefly, and then pushed his office door open. "Mr. Ross, I hope I'm not interrupting you, but I just thought that you deserve some sort of explanation of what's been going on with me this week." He motioned for me to take a seat opposite his massive desk. As I made myself comfortable, he said,

"Yes, Nancy, I've been getting worried about you. Are you feeling homesick?" That question took me by surprise, and I laughed before saying,

"No sir, I'm not homesick at all! In fact, I love it here! You're making me into a true Texan."

"Well, you know you can't be called a true Texan until you have at least two pairs of cowboy boots in your closet," he stated as he brought both feet out from under his desk to show me a new pair of boots that he had bought the week before.

"I guess I'll have to go shopping soon," I replied. "I wasn't aware that was a requirement of this state!" He laughed his deep, throaty chuckle, and said,

"Now tell me, what's been going on?" He moved from behind his desk to an armchair next to me. I decided this wouldn't be so hard, after all.

"I've been sleeping almost non-stop since our return

from Colorado," I began. He nodded his acknowledgement and motioned for me to continue. "I mean a *lot,* more than I have ever slept before—and I'm not even staying out late!"

He smiled, "I guess the mountains really sapped your strength, didn't they," he questioned.

"I guess they did, but my right hand and arm are numb now, too," I acknowledged. He looked at me quizzically, not understanding how those two symptoms might be related.

"Did you hurt it skiing?" he asked, reasonably enough.

"No, sir, I don't remember hurting it in any way, but it has a strange feeling, too."

"Nancy, I think you need to see a doctor about your arm, dear."

"As a matter of fact, I have an appointment with one this afternoon, and I'll need to leave work early.

"That's not a problem," he stated, "You can just work through lunch until you need to leave." He even encouraged me to leave work now, and simply come in a little early tomorrow. I thanked him, but said I would stay until 2:00 to finish some work from the day before, as well as to catch up on the work that had begun piling up because of my tardiness the last few days. He agreed, and I worked through the lunch break until it was time for me to leave.

Stephanie was a new employee at the company, and she volunteered to go with me to the appointment. I knew that she was just in the process of going through the orientation tapes, but I also remembered how mind-numbingly boring they were. I don't know why I agreed to let her drive me to my appointment, but in retrospect, I'm awfully glad that I did. Stephanie followed me to my apartment, where I left my car, and we proceeded to the appointment.

Luckily, Stephanie was a calming presence for me, as she filled out all the new patient forms for me. I had lost the ability to write intelligibly a few days before. The office was not a terribly busy one, and I was called to an exam room about twenty minutes after three, to meet the doctor.

Dr. Watkins was a man in his fifties, balding, kindly, and very thorough. After telling him of my symptoms and a brief exam, he immediately placed a call to the Radiology Department,

"This is Dr. Watkins," he said abruptly to whoever answered the phone. "I have a patient here that needs a CT scan immediately" he spoke with urgency to his voice.

The answer came over the speaker phone, "I'm sorry, Dr. Watkins, but we are so behind schedule today."

"This is an emergency," Dr. Watkins insisted. "I have patient in urgent need of this scan!" Without waiting for an answer, he continued, "Tell Dr. Robbins that I said exceptions must be made. We are coming now." Stephanie later told me that she heard him tell his nurse that he was afraid they might discover "something very bad" from the scan, which explained the lack of color in her face when I saw her as the doctor wheeled me in a wheelchair to Radiology.

Not a nurse, but the doctor *himself* took me to Radiology, which I thought was a little bit too hands-on, but whatever rocked his boat was fine with me. I quite simply wanted some answers to the questions that nobody had reasonable answers for!

With the doctor's presence in Radiology, they found time for my CT scan promptly, and I was receiving the scan within 15 minutes of arriving in the department. When I emerged, the doctor was nowhere to be seen and an orderly from the hospital wheeled me back to the doctor's office. I waited for what seemed to be hours, but was only 45 minutes, for Dr. Watkins to come into his office.

He asked me if there was anyone in the waiting room with me. I answered that a work colleague had brought me to the appointment and would be taking me home. The doctor asked for her name, then had a nurse bring Stephanie into his office to sit with me. I thought nothing of this, and welcomed Stephanie into the inner circle. The doctor then sat down behind his massive desk, cleared his throat a few times, and he began speaking. At this point, I was in the room, but felt as though I was watching everything from a distance. Even the doctor's voice sounded muffled to me.

"Well, Nancy, the CT scan showed us just what I thought it would". He paused for dramatic effect before saying, "It showed us some masses in your brain. Now I don't want to alarm you, but I've spoken to Dr. Wellbourne and he wants to see you in his office tomorrow."

My head was spinning as he explained in his muffled voice that Dr. Wellbourne was a neurosurgeon and he agreed to see me tomorrow as a favor to Dr. Watkins. I guess I should have acted more enthusiastic at the news, but in reality, I was trying to focus on his face because the room had now started spinning out of control. I tried to be polite as I gathered my purse in one hand and unsteadily stood from the chair I was sitting. Dr. Watkins handed Stephanie his business card after he scribbled something on the back of it. I was already to the door, anxious to get to my apartment.

Stephanie led me by the arm to her car in the parking garage. As we walked slowly down the halls, neither Stephanie nor I said a word. I don't remember speaking until we got to my apartment. I can't remember exactly what I said, but it was something along the lines of, will you help me tell my parents? I didn't want her to leave me. I needed someone there to help me figure out a way to tell my parents that I needed brain surgery. This was the single-most, difficult thing with which I had ever been faced…until now.

I called their office first, but they had already closed for the day. I tried calling them at home, but I just got the answering machine. I was aware that it takes about 15 minutes to get from their office to our home in the country, but I also knew that mom often went to the grocery store or post office before leaving town. I began to panic, knowing that I wouldn't be able to reach them easily.

This was 1986, and cell phones were not the norm. Out of desperation, I called my oldest sister, whom I knew would be home from her job as a sixth-grade teacher. I didn't know if mom and dad had even mentioned my symptoms to her or not. This wasn't the time to go into long detail with her, so I just blurted out with,

"Have you seen mom or dad?!" She sounded surprised.

I don't know if I sounded panic-stricken, or what she was thinking, but she replied very calmly.

"Hi, Nancy. They will be home soon, what's the matter?" in her matter of fact tone of voice, but I could tell that she was suspicious that something was wrong.

"Never mind, just find them for me, okay?" I practically bit her head off; I was so stressed by the afternoon's events. Before I could hang up, I heard dad's voice in the background. He had just happened to stop by her house to visit with the grandchildren before going the mile down the road to home. Jacque was saying,

"Dad, come talk to Nancy. I think something's wrong." Jacque sounded irritated.

As soon as I heard Dad's voice on the other end of the line, I burst into tears. I don't know if it was the sound of his voice, or knowing that he cared what was happening to me, but just hearing his voice at the other end of the phone line took all my defenses away. Suddenly, this was not happening to someone else, but I was telling him what the doctor had told me *in the first person.*

It all became very real to me. I need surgery to remove whatever it was in my head that is causing all my problems. I relayed the doctor's visit to dad in detail as best I could between sobs. He took all the information, processed it as best he could, and calmly told me to settle down. Normally that type of remark would have made me angry. *(Don't tell me to settle down, just help me know what to do so this "thing" can be fixed.)* He said he would go home, talk to mom, and we would all decide what we should do together.

As he hung up the phone, he told me that he loved

me, and that he would call as soon as he and mom had a plan. Just knowing that I would soon have a plan to follow, and that my parents would be with me through it all, was enough to make me "settle down". I told Stephanie to go home to her husband, while I lay on the couch with a room-darkening mask over my eyes in the silence of my apartment. About 30 minutes later my phone rang. I hesitated to answer it because I wasn't ready to face reality yet. I thought it may be one of my friends, calling to ask how the doctor's visit had gone.

After several rings, I reluctantly picked up the phone. To my relief, it was my mom, and she said she and dad were coming down to see me ASAP. I knew that Arkadelphia was about a four-and-a-half-hour drive from Dallas. I also knew that my dad would most likely speed on the way. So, taking all this into account, I assumed I would be seeing them in three hours or so. As I was lying on the couch, trying not to think of brain surgery or anything in the future, someone knocked on my door.

I opened the door to find Dave. Stephanie had called him to tell him what was going on with me because she thought a familiar face would help me at this time. As a relatively new member of our Account Reps team, she was unaware of the history Dave and I shared. She had simply noticed his name and phone number on a pad I kept beside the phone and took it upon herself to call him when she left my apartment.

I hadn't seen him in about four months, so I was surprised to see him outside my door. I opened the door and stepped back so Dave could get inside. He stepped toward me, hesitantly, as though he wasn't sure of what to do. I laughed a nervous type of laugh, and said,

"Wow, I didn't expect to see you here again," as I leaned forward to give him a hug.

I thought that there would be something familiar to the hug, but I felt nothing. In fact, it was a rather tense, robotic type of hug, if robots hug. It did not feel familiar to me at all, which was a relief to me. We sat on the couch, not touching,

"Someone named Stephanie called this afternoon," he stated. "She said she works with you."

"Yes, she does, but why did she call *you*," I asked suspiciously.

"She told me about your doctor's appointment this afternoon. I guess she didn't want you to be home alone," Dave replied softly.

"Well, she shouldn't have called you," I replied with more than a little bitterness in my voice. "This is my problem, and I really don't know why she called you in the first place."

"I thought you might need a hug," Dave said quietly. "I'm sorry, Nance," using the moniker by which he had called me for 9 years. "I guess I should have just called instead." His voice was almost a whisper in the silent apartment.

"No, don't mind me, I'm just a girl who has just been told she needs brain surgery," I said as I fell into his arms, crying. This time, his arms felt familiar as he wrapped them around me while gently rocking me back and forth. We stayed in this position until my tears stopped. I did not want him seeing me feel sorry for myself. I decided at that moment not to let anyone see me feeling sorry for myself. We talked about mundane things, I even asked how his father was doing, and he asked the same of my family.

"I'll be fine," I said as I wiped my tears from my face.

"I know you will," he said, as he started to stand and walk toward the door. "Call me if you need anything." I know he just added the last part to make himself feel better, to at least offer assistance of some kind. It was 11 years before I spoke to him again.

After he left, I really didn't know what I should do. Wandering aimlessly around my apartment, I noticed that Stephanie had begun packing a suitcase for me, so I started where she had left off. I packed my nightshirt, robe, and slippers, as well as a few casual outfits such as a navy blue sweat suit, a red one, and some extra t-shirts, when there was a knock on my door.

Who could it be this time, I wondered? My hopes skyrocketed for an instant before I realized it was way too early for my parents to have made the trip already. I was already feeling let down, as I opened the door. Amazingly, my parents were standing at my doorstep! I threw the door open and fell into their waiting arms. It was such a relief to have them in town, at my apartment, with me, that the tears began flowing from each of us as they had never flowed before. All I could say was, "You're here-- you're here!" between sobs as they made their way into my apartment.

After my hysterical sobbing was over, I remembered Dr. Watkins' business card on my table. Stephanie had placed it there when she brought me home from the doctor. On the back was the doctor's home phone number.

He had given that to Stephanie and told her to have my parents call him when they got to town. I handed the card to my mom, and told her to call the doctor. She handed the card to my dad. I found a notepad and pen for dad to write with, and the three of us held our breath while he punched the numbers into the phone.

Dad introduced himself when the doctor answered the phone, and started writing on the paper. Mostly, dad was just listening. The doctor explained what the scan had shown, what tests I needed to have performed, and then I saw dad draw a circle, about the size of a nickel. I thought he was just doodling, and then he wrote the numbers 4-5 beside the circle. And then he embarrassed me. He stopped writing momentarily, to ask the doctor,

"Is there any possible way that we can take Nancy back to Arkansas for treatment there?"

I immediately froze in my movements. He told the doctor that he wanted to take me back to Arkansas for treatment there?! I was stunned into silence. *What was he thinking? Doesn't he know the doctors in Dallas are far superior to the doctors in Arkansas? There was no way that he was going to take me out of Texas.* (You see, I considered myself a true Texan by this time, even without the boots and as such, thought that everything was bigger and better in Texas.)

As my mind raced a million miles an hour, I watched as dad wrote the initials MRI on the notepad beside the nickel-sized circle he had drawn earlier. *What was that?* He listened to the doctor for another few minutes, and then he thanked the doctor, and hung up the phone.

It was not until this moment that I began wondering

how my parents had gotten to Dallas in such a short amount of time. It turns out that my mom had an intuition that something was seriously wrong with me, and had packed their bags for Dallas the night before. She had then made several calls around my hometown, and found someone to fly them here in a private plane. This shocked me because my dad has never particularly liked flying - even on commercial airlines. He always says that it messes with his ears and makes it hard to hear for about a week after flying, so we usually make a road trip out of any destination. But first, I wanted to know what the doctor had said. Dad looked me in the eyes and said,

"Nan, it doesn't look good, but he told me the name of a certain type of x-ray that you need, and if we can find one in Arkansas, he doesn't see any need to stay here," Dad told us.

He then looked at my mom and said, "Now it's your job to find this X-ray in Arkansas so we can take her home."

I sat wordlessly as dad explained that the masses Dr. Watkins had seen on my brain were approximately nickel-sized, and there were at least four to five of them, which explained the cryptic notes he had written on the notepad. Mom began phoning her friends in Arkansas that might know something about an MRI, good neurologists, etc. She remembered that a hospital in Little Rock had just received a new MRI a few weeks before, where it had made the front page of the statewide newspaper.

I was doubtful that it was the same thing the doctor had spoken of, but she called my aunt in Little Rock, who confirmed that it was the same thing the doctor had mentioned. My aunt volunteered at the University of Arkansas Medical Science Center, so she knew a little bit about the new x-ray. That's it. She told mom it was indeed an MRI so my parents were relieved to hear they could take me back to Arkansas.

I was still doubtful about going back to Arkansas. I honestly thought that going back to Arkansas was equivalent to a death sentence for me! The next morning, the three of us loaded into my Buick Regal and headed for Arkansas. Even though I was doubtful about going home, I climbed into the back seat.

I slept most of the way, and when I woke up, the car was turning into the familiar driveway of home. My symptoms had spread. My right foot was numb and had the same prickly feeling as my hand and arm. Mom and Dad helped me to my room, and I don't think that anything has ever felt as safe and comforting as my bed in my childhood bedroom at that point in my life. I slept the rest of that afternoon, finally waking in time for dinner. Mom had been on the phone all day, finding a neurologist with room for a new patient.

After making several calls, getting referrals from doctors, as well as referrals from friends, mom managed to get me in to see a neurosurgeon in Little Rock the next week. This gave mom and dad comfort, but I was still leery of the entire "Little Rock doctors can be just as good as doctors in Dallas" mindset that seemed to have overtaken my parents.

I don't remember much of that week passing by, I know that I slept a lot, and then went back for more sleep. Even as a teen with mono, I don't remember ever sleeping so much. My days consisted of eating and sleeping, and not much else. I had contacted Mr. Ross after my appointment that gave me the news of the masses in my brain, and informed him that my parents had brought me back to Arkansas. Mr. Ross agreed that I was where I needed to be.

"Nancy, you just take care of yourself," Mr. Ross told me. "Don't worry about your districts here. I'll take care of them for you, in the meantime just concentrate on getting better. We will see you in a few weeks when you get back."

With that said, I hung up the telephone and put the deadlines that had been on my mind since I had left Dallas out of my mind, being assured that my job would be waiting for me when I returned.

THE FINAL VERDICT
– A LIFE SENTENCE

T he day came for my appointment. Mom and I went to Little Rock, and by this time my symptoms had spread further along my right side, encompassing my entire right side from my head to my toes. I was having difficulty walking as you might assume, and even was slurring my speech somewhat. All I knew was that I wanted this thing taken out of my head, and have my scalp sewn back so that I could start growing hair again.

I had come to terms with the loss of my hair that would accompany brain surgery. That bit didn't faze me at all. At this point, all I knew was that something was inside me, and I wanted it out! To me, brain surgery was the shortest way to getting back to my normal life. I mainly went to this appointment knowing I would need surgery, I just was anxious to have it over with.

My mom and I waited nervously in the doctor's office while patients with varying amounts of hair loss came and went. Most women covered their heads with scarves or hats, and one lady with a smile on her face sported a jaunty beret. Mom and I waited patiently for my name to be called; all the while watching as the parade of patients limped, rolled, or were otherwise assisted across the floor when their names were called. Suddenly I didn't feel as self-conscience about my slight limp. After perusing the medical magazines, I was called into the doctor's office, and after the Dr. Hayes examined me, he sat down in a chair across from me and said with confidence,

"I don't think you have a brain tumor in the least." I think the he was waiting for some exclamations of relief from my mom and me. We gave him puzzled looks instead.

The room was silent as I looked at my mother with an "I told you so" expression. My mom stammered,

"Wh-what do you mean?" I could tell that she was thinking it might be something far worse.

"I mean that nobody can give you a diagnosis based on one CT scan and an examination." He went on to say that I needed to be admitted to a local hospital for more testing, and then he said those all too familiar words that would become a part of my daily vocabulary for years to come.

"Nancy needs an MRI of her brain, and we can go from there. Can you get her checked into to St. Vincent's this afternoon?"

I was trying with everything I had to focus on the words he was saying, but to be honest; he was too handsome to simply listen to his words. His eyelashes were of a length that is only seen in mascara commercials, and his eyes are a deep green color, which when I looked at them more closely had flecks of yellow in them, that made his eyes seem to dance around the room as he looked from mom to myself.

I wasn't even aware of his words to me, as mom anxiously reached for her purse as she stood to leave the doctor's office. I was limping alongside in the very awkward gait that had become my normal way of walking. I was also holding on to things to help me balance: chairs, desks, tables, doors, walls, anything that would give some sense of stability. My right leg was dragging quite a bit, also. Strangely enough, that aspect didn't concern me as much as the never-ending pain that I felt on my entire right side.

What at first had started as a feeling of being pricked by pins had now elevated to daggers being plunged into my arms and legs, as well as losing motor control of my right hand and arm. Each separate pain almost took my breath away as I concentrated on walking. Each doctor that I saw put me through the standard neurological tests to measure my ability to grasp things, lift arms and legs, touch fingers to nose, and so on. I noticed that the later in the day I was asked to perform these tasks, the lesser my ability was to complete them.

One such exercise that I repeatedly failed was sitting in a chair with my arms straight above my head. With my eyes closed, I was told to lower my arms to my lap. I don't think anyone was as surprised as I was when my right arm practically fell into my lap. Dr. Hayes just smiled knowingly, told us not to be too alarmed by the events that had just taken place, go check into the hospital, and he would come by my room later to see us. Of course, the moment we were out of the doctor's earshot, I turned to mom and said,

"See? *Please* will you take me back to Dallas? At least the doctors there knew what they were looking at!"

"Nancy, just calm down," mom said. "I need to talk to your dad before we decide anything."

I decided to let that 'calm down' remark slide this time, we were both under a lot of stress in this field of unknowing that had enveloped our lives since I had been informed only a week prior to this day that I had several masses in my brain. *Had it really only been a week?* Little did I suspect how my life would change forever in the coming weeks, months, and yes, years.

We went to a cafeteria inside a local mall before we went to the hospital. I sat with a tall glass of sweet iced tea that Southerners are known to enjoy, Mom had her coffee, and we shared a piece of pie, while mom made phone calls to her sister, my Aunt Nancy whom I was named after, and my dad. After relaying the doctor's orders, both my aunt and my dad thought that I should just go ahead and be admitted to the hospital. They obviously had more faith in the doctor than I did!

We left the cafeteria after about an hour, maybe more. Mom had convinced me to go into the hospital that night. I don't know what made me abandon the notion that Dallas was where I needed to be, I just remember being tired and wanting to lie down in a bed. I would have preferred my bed at home, but at this point a hospital bed would have to do.

After I was admitted to the hospital, mom headed home. She said she would be back the next day. I told her not to worry about me, just to call and let me know when she would be back. She looked as though she had aged twenty years that day.

For the first time, I thought about all this from her perspective. I'm sure it wasn't easy for her to hear a neurologist explain what kind of tests needed to be performed on her daughter, and just as hard waiting for a diagnosis. My dad had stayed in Arkadelphia to run the business, so it was just mom and myself seeing the doctor that day.

I would have slept soundly that night had I not been in a hospital. I know I was awakened at least five or six times that night by nurses just checking on me. I had always heard people say that if you want peace and quiet, don't be admitted to a hospital. I believed them after my first night there. Luckily, Dr. Hayes had prescribed something to help me sleep.

I was beyond exhausted by this time, it didn't take long to fall asleep, even with the sound of footsteps in the hall, carts with squeaky wheels, and the constant messages being broadcast over the PA system. A nurse came to wake me around 6:30 the next morning, followed by additional blood work, taking my vital signs, etc. I told the nurse that I didn't sleep very well the night before, so could I rest a little more? She thought I was joking at first, and laughed. I assured her that no, I wasn't teasing and I was still sleepy. She turned off the overhead light when she left. Just as I was getting comfortable once again, my phone rang.

It was mom, and she was on her way to Little Rock to see me. She asked if the doctor had been in yet, and when

I answered in the negative, she said she hoped to be there when he came. Next came the typical question of,

"How did you sleep last night?"

I laughed half-heartedly and said,

"You wouldn't believe me if I told you!"

She arrived in my room in a little over an hour. In the meantime, I ate my hospital breakfast, watched the Today show, and waited for my doctor to come. I was anxious to get the tests started, so that I could go back to Dallas and return to my single life and friends. The doctor came by mid-morning.

Dr. Hayes was going through the now all-too-familiar neurological motor skills testing with me when mom came in the room. As hard as I tried, I could not smile with a symmetrical smile, I also could not bring my arms down to my lap in a slow, continuous motion, and I definitely couldn't stand on one leg!

One other test required me to touch my nose, then touch the doctor's index finger while he stood in front of me, changing the location of his finger each time I touched my nose. It sounds almost like a game you would play with babies, but it was hard! He later told me that he was testing my eye movement, their tracking ability, and to see if I was having difficulty with spatial differences. He also tested the strength in my grip, and arms, by having me stand with my arms outstretched while he pushed down on them. I could tell that my results were worse than the day before, and wondered what that meant.

"Hm-m-m" the doctor said. "I'm still not convinced that you have a brain tumor at all."

I looked over at mom as if to say, *NOW,* will you take

me to Dallas?! She just shook her head slightly, and asked the doctor,

"What do we do now?" She was prepared to do anything the doctor suggested, and quite frankly I would have jumped through flaming hoops if it were requested of me!

"We give her an MRI next," the Dr. Hayes said. "That will tell me a little more about the lesions. Let me set her up with an MRI as soon as possible." Dr. Hayes explained further what was so special about an MRI, that it would take x-rays of my brain in layers, so that the doctor could see how large the lesions were, the depth of them per se. It was basically an x-ray that would show the depth of the lesions, instead of just the size of them. We thanked him as he left the room, not knowing when this mysterious MRI would take place, but hoping it would give the doctor the answers he was looking for- and us too.

By now it was time for lunch. Mom went down to the cafeteria to eat a chicken salad sandwich that she said was only partially soggy. I don't know if she was telling the truth or not, or trying to make me feel better about the hospital food! Nevertheless, I ate my lunch eagerly, as the steroids I had been taking over the past week and a half were causing my appetite to skyrocket. I was *always* hungry these days, and sleepy.

Not long after the lunch tray was cleared away, my great-aunt came to visit me, bringing a gift. It was a book about the power of prayer in healing cancer and other ailments. I began reading the book as mom and my great-aunt made their way down to the cafeteria for coffee. I fell asleep while reading the book, and the next thing I remember a nurse was waking me, saying the ambulance was ready to take me for the MRI. These machines were so new to the medical establishments in Arkansas that three area hospitals had pooled their money together and shared one machine between them.

I recall very little about the actual MRI that followed. I remember it was a huge machine, taking up almost the entire space of one room. The attendants lay me on the table, then slowly slid me into the machine until only my feet remained visible to the technicians. If you have never had one of the earliest MRIs, it is similar to being put into a metal coffin, being sealed shut, and then being subjected to what seemed like extremely loud pounding on the outside of the machine until the sound reverberated through every bone in my body. The whole thing lasted about an hour and a half, or maybe more.

I lost track of time during the MRI and the technicians told me afterward that they could tell I was getting impatient. Apparently, my feet were showing my impatience by tapping against one another with increasing frequency as the time ticked on. The technician could speak to me via a speaker in the machine, so at least I wasn't entirely cut off from communication.

I felt like a pizza being pushed into an oven when the technician shoved me head-first into the massive machine. I remember trying to count to 1000 by twos, threes, anything to help make the time pass more quickly. At times, my feet would become so agitated that the technician would have to ask me to calm down, and assure me that it wouldn't be much longer- which I quickly discovered was a relative term!

After almost two hours inside the makeshift tomb, I was returned to my hospital room, where my mom and Aunt Tiddley were waiting to hear all about this new x-ray I'd just had. As I was wheeled into my room, I recall seeing Aunt Tiddley and mentioning that I felt sorry for older people who may have to undergo the same experience. My great aunt took that to mean that I must have spent the two hours I was gone thinking of elderly patients going through the same thing. Actually, I was simply remarking just how terrible the experience had been for me! My comment wasn't nearly as selfless as she made it out to be.

That night, I was visited by my college roommate and her husband, as well as a couple of guys from the fraternity for which I was a Little Sister while at Fayetteville. Mom had been sitting with me, so she excused herself to go get coffee while we talked. About 30 minutes after she left, my room phone rang and it was the neurosurgeon who had ordered the MRI. My friends visited quietly while I listened silently as he told me that he had seen the results of the MRI and he would be in tomorrow morning to talk to us. He then proceeded to tell me that he had some good news for me, and that I didn't have a brain tumor! This was another case of a term being taken as relative. *Why was it good news that I couldn't have surgery to fix the problem in my brain?!*

He proceeded to tell me that I could relax, but the scans showed evidence of Multiple Sclerosis. Dr. Hayes then said good night, and I was left to deal with a room full of visitors and a head full of information that I wasn't quite ready to comprehend or share. My friends left soon after the phone call ended. I told mom about the call from

Dr. Hayes when she got back from the cafeteria. She said MS is what Mari Martin was diagnosed with a few years earlier.

Mari's father was once the District Superintendent for the United Methodist Churches in the Arkadelphia District. Mari and I had become good friends while they lived in Arkadelphia several years before. Mari was a year older than me, and she had a sister a year younger. Our parents had become good friends, and while I had not kept in touch with Mari, our moms had. I told mom she should call Anna (Mari's mom) before the doctor came to see us in the morning. She promptly called Mari's parents and wrote down several questions to ask him when he saw us.

The next morning, Dr. Hayes came in my room sporting a very jovial attitude.

"Did Nancy tell you the good news?" he asked mom. I answered for her,

"Yes, I told her, but I don't really understand what is so good about it". The sullenness in my voice surprised even me. *Am I really that spoiled?*

At this point I had pretty much resigned myself to neurosurgery being in my future. Yes, it kind of freaked me out, but I was of the mindset that the doctors would shave my head, open my skull, and remove the masses that had shown up on my MRI, then they would close my head, my hair would grow back, and I would go back to my apartment and life in Dallas. Simple, right? At least that's how I had it worked out in my mind. But like the saying from Robert Burns says, "the best laid plans of mice and men often go astray". Such was how it went with my plans, from that point on.

Dr. Hayes proceeded to give us a very rosy outlook on life with MS, but since we already knew someone with the disease, we knew the ups as well as the downs with this disease. Of course, each person with MS experiences varying symptoms. For example, Mari had lost the eyesight in one or both of her eyes multiple times. I dreaded the same thing would happen to me, and each night I thanked God for allowing me to keep my eyesight.

We had an appointment the next day with a neurologist across town. Dr. Gaines' office was located in a contemporary office building made mostly of windows. The interior was typical medical office décor with chairs scattered around the perimeter as well as out of date medical periodicals for the patients' reading enjoyment.

We signed in and the receptionist handed me what looked like a stack of 12 papers to fill out. Mom busied herself with the paperwork because I couldn't even hold a pen in my hand, much less write intelligibly. Luckily, she said she didn't mind doing all of the writing because it gave her something to do.

"Besides, they don't even have a *Reader's Digest* for normal people," she said with a smile.

"Are you calling yourself normal now?" was my response. It was so tiring, just waiting for my name to be called. Each time the door to what I assumed was the passage to the examining rooms opened, I would look up expectantly, waiting for my name. I soon came to the realization that the building was home to 6 neurologists. That gave me some sense of relief, realizing that not every patient in the waiting room had MS. I mean, they could be here because of anything! Migraines, head injuries, recovering from strokes, all of these would be a cause for neurologists' appointments.

The moment that I realized this fact, I breathed a deep sigh of relief, only to immediately say a silent prayer for all the patients in the waiting room. After all, a diagnosis of MS was huge to me, but what if some other patient was finding out that their tumor is malignant! While my eyes were closed in prayer my name was finally called. I looked at mom as she stood to follow the nurse. She had a brave face on, and I just hoped my face was just as brave. Instead, I knew it showed just how terrified I felt as I fell in line behind the nurse.

Dr. Gaines was about my mom's age, and it turned out that he had received his undergraduate degree from Henderson State in Arkadelphia! He and mom conversed about that similarity for a moment, discovering that they attended at around the same time, although mom pointed out that she was several years ahead of him! With that out of the way, mom felt much more relaxed and that feeling continued onto me as well. Dr. Gaines began going through the standard neurological tests with me, which I promptly failed!

He took meticulous notes in my file, noting the amount of weakness in each test. It was tiring, but Dr. Gaines said that I showed results typical of a person with MS, which he meant to be comforting to me, but there was still so much about MS that I didn't know.

Of course, he also gave us a positive outlook on the diagnosis of Multiple Sclerosis. I recall him saying,

"They are researching this disease each day, and I'm convinced they will have a cure within months, if not years." Those words gave me such encouragement in the first years of living with MS. I suppose they still offer me some semblance of hope, but after 31 years of waiting for a cure, I'm a little more jaded.

In a perfect world, these types of statements would be true, but we don't live in a perfect world. I believe that doctors should be careful to not make such broad generalized statements, because it can give a false hope and that sometimes is worse than accepting the actual truth.

Looking back on it now, I can see that I lived in denial of the diagnosis for years. Of course, I didn't know that I was in denial. I thought I was handling my diagnosis well, judging by what friends and acquaintances were saying. Often, the first thing someone says to me is, "You're so brave." And the next thing they say is something along the lines of, "But you don't look sick!" which is often true. Fortunately, the outside world cannot see the pain MS causes on a daily basis.

MS is a chronic disease, but many people with MS choose to suffer in silence. How many friends do you know who would gladly listen to the daily lists of complaints each day? I think that is why a lot of people with MS simply suck it all in instead of complaining about each and every ache and pain. Who wants to be *that* friend?! This is why MS can be a life sentence, because for many it is a slow social death which eventually isolates them from their social circles, which can often act as a life preserver when the ship begins to sink.

MAKING LEMONADE,
AND WAITING

D r. Gaines had told me that he couldn't give me a positive diagnosis of MS until I'd experienced two or more exacerbations. So now I resigned myself to sitting and waiting for the next exacerbation, kind of. I returned to my job in Dallas with the constant nagging sensation that another exacerbation was in my future in the back of my mind. That was something that never completely left my head.

The thought continued to hang around in the back of my mind, kind of like an annoying mosquito that won't stop buzzing in your ear as you attempt to read a good book. It was a nuisance to me. That's all. I thought I was handling it well, when in actuality, I was living in denial.

I had decided to start making healthier choices in my eating habits on a daily basis. I had read in a brochure from the National MS Society that stated whole foods are preferred over processed foods for the diets of MS patients, so I started eating healthier than I had been, and cooking healthy meals for myself. No more fast food for me! I was becoming a decent cook, if I do say so myself.

I had stopped jogging after work, which was a shame because the apartment complex I was in boasted a large community of walkers/joggers. The fact is that I stopped jogging after one day when I had made myself too exhausted and barely made it back to my apartment after my daily jog on one of the many trails provided for exercise.

It frightened me, to think that I could collapse on a trail and no one would know. I scared myself that day, and stopped jogging. Some days I would still go for a walk after work to decompress after a stressful day. The wooded walking trails provided reminded me of Arkansas in a way. I could walk away my stress and forget I was in a busy metropolis. Of course, I could still hear the traffic going by, but if I pulled my visor over my eyes, and turned on my tunes, I could almost forget I was in Dallas. It became a sort of refuge to me. The breeze through the pine trees helped take the hard edges off the busy life I had made for myself.

Often on these trails, I found myself longing for the comforts of my hometown. I went home for the July 4th weekend celebration that my family always holds for family and friends at our pond. The pond itself is about 7 acres that my dad dug out in one of his pastures. He had been telling us for years that he wanted to build a pond at this particular spot where numerous underground springs could maintain the water level for fish. I don't think any of us in the family could have imagined what a large project it would become.

The pond is our family's spring, summer, and fall gathering place for fishing, canoeing, paddle boating, swimming and general relaxation. The grandkids and great-grandkids have all grown up here, partaking in the many outdoor activities, well as the abundance of food, sunshine, and memories provided there. Dad had the help of his three sons in law while finishing a small, one room cabin with a bathroom and a long kitchen cabinet with a sink with running water and for prepping meals and cleanup.

As a family, we named the pond and adjoining cabin and outdoor fireplace, WaHiMoWay, taking the first few letters from each of our last names: Wasson, Hill, Morgan and Wayland. Carol came up with this inventive name one day while we were all there enjoying it.

The pond, as it is collectively referred, sits on 40 acres off the paved main road in our small community. It is surrounded by all varieties of trees: Elm, Sweet Gum, Oak, Pine, and Dogwood to name a few.

There is a wooden dock jutting into the center of the pond, from which the kids of all ages enjoy jumping into the cool water during the heat of the summer. I consider it an oasis.

I returned to my apartment and job in Dallas after celebrating the 4th with my family. The initial shock of my diagnosis with Multiple Sclerosis was wearing off by this time, and I think that I was managing this disease quite well.

I was cautious about what types of food I ate, and kept the amount of processed foods I ingest each day to a minimum. That meant no more fast food burgers and fries for me, which was a smart move if I have MS or not. I noticed that it didn't make that much difference in my daily life, but it sure didn't hurt, so eating this way became my daily routine. I had grown up eating the home-grown vegetables from our gardens back home, and I quickly included all kinds of produce and vegetables into my daily menus.

I returned home to Arkadelphia one weekend in late August. On Sunday, I was extremely tired after church, so I started back to Dallas soon after enjoying lunch with my family. It had been a relaxing weekend, and promised to be a relaxing drive back to the Dallas/Fort Worth metropolis.

At the time, I was driving a blue 1984 Buick Regal that my Mom and Dad had purchased for me while I was in college at the University of Arkansas in Fayetteville. This car was my favorite car because it accelerated like a dream down the highway and rode smoothly, much like a boat on a calm lake. I remember setting the cruise control on my car for the drive on I-30 West, and not even touching the accelerator or brake until I was approaching my exit in Dallas four and a half hours later.

I looked up from where I had been adjusting my radio, and realized that my exit was quickly approaching. *Too* quickly! To my shock, I also noticed the exit ramp was full of cars. Trying to move my foot onto the brake was futile. It felt stuck to the floorboard. Panic began rising in me. *What to do? Is this how I will die?* Fortunately, there was plenty of space between me and the car ahead, but my car wasn't slowing down in the least.

"Oh, God, please help me," I muttered aloud to no one in particular, but in retrospect it *was* directed to someone in particular, God! I managed to think clearly enough to take the cruise control off and place my right foot onto the floorboard and that made my car stop accelerating, but I had been going 67 miles an hour, and I was quickly approaching the bumper of the Nissan Maxima ahead of me! I don't know how it happened, but somehow my car came to stop just inches from hitting the bumper ahead of me.

I left several yards of rubber on the exit ramp that day. I don't remember closing my eyes at the impending impact, but as my car slowed to a stop, I raised my eyes to the cars ahead of me. Looking around at all the drivers and passengers staring at me through the windshields of their respective vehicles with varying looks of disinterest or disgust, I let my head rest on my steering wheel while my heart and mind were reeling.

Once I felt my car stop, I looked down at my legs and saw that both feet were on the brake pedal. I have no idea how they got there, and I began shaking uncontrollably, almost convulsively. At this point traffic began moving forward slowly and I turned my car into the nearest parking lot to get some sort of control over myself and my emotions. As I was sitting in the parking lot, another car pulled beside me. The driver, a middle-aged woman with a modern hairstyle rolled down her passenger side window, and asked,

"Are you all right, dear?" the woman was peering into my eyes, and seemed genuinely concerned.

"I saw what just happened back there," gesturing with her head at the exit ramp behind us. "I'll get you some water, you just wait right here 'til I get back, okay hon?"

With that, she pulled ahead of my car and into the drive-thru lane that I noticed was right where my car was idling. I took two or three deep breaths and began mentally going over the events of the last 5 minutes. I was still shaking, and it came to mind that I had very narrowly escaped death just moments earlier. I began crying inconsolably as I realized that my life wasn't the only one saved that day.

What would have happened to the drivers and passengers in the other cars had my car not stopped when it did? At that time, the kind lady that had spoken to me earlier returned, holding two medium sized cups filled with ice and water. She held one out to me saying,

"I don't know about you, dear, but I need something to drink! I didn't want to take the time to find a bar nearby..." she said while chuckling to herself at the comment. I smiled and nodded my head in agreement. She continued talking to me, but I was still in a state of shock so I merely smiled in agreement as I took the cup of water from her. Until the water touched my lips, I hadn't realized just how thirsty I had become.

I leaned back in my seat and began gulping the water as if I had just walked through a desert. She was still rambling on about trivial things, such as the traffic and the weather. I honestly could not seem to focus on the one-sided conversation, and simply nodded whenever she paused in her discourse. After I had my fill of the refreshing water, I wiped my mouth on my sleeve and expressed my gratefulness to her.

"Don't think a thing about it, hon," she said as she stood patting my arm. "I don't know if you believe in miracles or not, but I sure do, and I just witnessed a miracle when your car stopped," she stated as she leaned into my car to hug me. "I *do* believe in miracles, and I know that's what kept you alive," I agreed with her as I covered her hand with my own. We remained frozen in the moment, locking eyes. Her deep brown eyes filled with tears as I whispered,

"Thank you" as I watched her turn and walk back to her car I knew that God had plans for me, I am not sure of what they are, or where they will take me.

I regret that I didn't have the common sense to introduce myself to her or even to ask her name. I honestly believe she was an angel sent from above to help calm my nerves. I think we encounter angels on a daily basis as we go about our everyday lives. They masquerade as ordinary people that come into our lives just when we need them. God is so good.

We said our goodbyes and went our separate ways, with me making my way cautiously toward my apartment complex, because the last thing I wanted was a repeat of the previous situation. I honestly didn't even notice my feet, which was a good thing. They weren't tingling, or in pain in any way, but they felt as though I was wearing three or four pairs of thick, wool hunting socks on each of my feet. I didn't dwell on this feeling, as I was focused on maneuvering through the typical Dallas traffic to the safety of my apartment. As I pulled my car into the parking lot, I noticed that my upstairs neighbors were driving behind me.

Rick and Scott lived in the apartment above mine, and we had become casual acquaintances over the past couple of months since they had moved in. I opened the car door to stand up, but suddenly was aware that my legs felt as sturdy as cooked noodles and there was no way that I would be able to stand!

Being as stubborn as I am, I determinedly swung my legs out my car door so that my shoes were touching the pavement. Then I attempted to pull myself to a standing position by holding onto the car door. I say that I *attempted* to do so, because the result was the exact opposite of standing...I found myself flat on my back in the hot parking lot! I called out to Rick as he and Scott made their way to the stairs,

"Rick! I need your help...can you and Scott help me?"

They rushed to my side as Scott was saying,

"Oh, my God! Where are you?"

I had slipped from visibility between cars in the parking lot. I didn't have the energy to laugh at Scott's statement until much later, after the three of us had made it to the stairs. They both rushed to my side and looked shocked to see me on the hot pavement, sandwiched between two cars.

"Hi guys, I need help getting to my door," I told them.

With that said, I was carried to my door by two handsome men! They had just finished playing basketball and were covered in sweat, but I didn't care. They could have been covered in anything and I would gratefully welcome their assistance. They carried me into my apartment and placed me on the couch. I then explained my MS diagnosis, and it turned out that Rick's mom also has MS, so for once I was receiving assistance from someone with experience with MS.

I am still amazed when God brings people into my life

just when they are needed. It turned out that Rick's mom was diagnosed with MS as an adult, and was still mobile. I don't know why that fact was so important to me, but it has become less important as time goes by. We talked for several more minutes, then they left to go meet some friends for dinner at a popular restaurant nearby. When they told me where they were going, my mouth started salivating,

"Oh, I just love Baja Louie's! They make the best chicken fajita salad with honey mustard dressing," I mentioned my favorite at the restaurant.

I lay back on my couch, and after assuring them that I didn't need anything, said goodbye to my heroes, not in shining armor, but heroes in sweaty basketball clothes. I fell asleep on the couch, exhausted beyond belief. I was awakened two hours later by knocking on my door. I was trying to wake up, attempting to figure out where I was and how I got there, when my apartment door opened. I didn't have time to react to the fact that a stranger was possibly walking into my apartment, when Rick stuck his head into the opening of the doorway and in his hands, was a bag of take-out from Baja Louie's.

"Nancy, we got this for you--we thought you may not feel like cooking tonight after the afternoon that you had," Rick placed the salad on the table. Tears filled my eyes for the third or fourth time that day, I gave Rick a hug, and said thank you for the millionth time. This time I remembered to lock the door after he left, walked to my couch, and ate the most delicious Chicken Fajita Salad I had ever eaten. That made twice in one day where God stepped in and provided me with things that I didn't know I needed, but definitely did! God is so good!

After eating the salad, I remembered to call mom and dad to make sure that they knew I had made it home to Dallas safely. I reluctantly told mom about the scare on the interstate, as well as the kindness expressed to me by the random lady who had brought the water.

"Well, I guess Dallas isn't as impersonal of a place to live after all," mom commented after I had recounted the frightening scene on I-30.

"But mom, just wait 'til I tell you everything that happened," I cut her off mid-sentence, then proceeded to tell her about my fall in the parking lot and my neighbors coming to my rescue

"Nancy, you have got to be more careful," mom admonished. When I finished telling her about my parking lot fall, and being rescued by my neighbors, and how increasingly tired I was becoming, mom sprang into action.

"Nancy, you get lots of rest tonight and then call me in the morning to let me know how you're feeling," mom was adamant about me resting well that night. How could I make her understand that these events didn't happen because I might have not rested well? Rest doesn't cure MS, it simply makes it more manageable at times.

"If you still feel badly in the morning, I'll just come down to get you," then we said our goodbyes and hung up the phones.

I immediately went to bed after brushing my teeth, and saying another prayer to God, thanking him for helping me get home today, and asking him to please not give me another exacerbation any time soon. I would love to tell you that I slept well that night, and awoke feeling refreshed. I didn't. The next morning, I awoke at 6:00, but was unable to walk at all!

I reached for my phone to make two early-morning phone calls: the first call was to my boss, telling him I wouldn't be in that day, and the next call was to my mom, whom was hoping I wasn't calling with bad news. Unfortunately, it was worse news. I called mom, and she said she was on her way. That's one thing about MS, you really can't plan on things happening a certain way for yourself. Life is that way, as is living with a diagnosis of MS! Woody Allen once said,

"If you want to make God laugh, tell him your plans!"

It makes me smile to think that God would allow to us make our plans, then allow Life to happen to us as He plans it! God already knows where our lives will take us. It is up to us to do something good with our lives. I guess I sound like some sort of Pollyanna when I mention, when life gives you lemons, make lemonade! I happen to think that's an important value on which to live, not matter your circumstances. I've been trying my hardest to make some of the most excellent lemonade for over 31 years now.

IS IT BRAVERY, OR JUST LIFE?

C an it truly be called bravery if you deal with whatever God chooses for you to deal with, or rather, however God chooses to test your faith? I was diagnosed with Multiple Sclerosis, and I deal with it... I simply don't see any other logical option! Some people have varying thoughts on God and dealing with chronic diseases. I happen to believe that God allows things to happen to us as a way of testing our faith, or belief in Him. I don't believe that God tests our belief in Him per se, but allows challenges to come to us, and then reassures us with His love.

This is my belief, and it doesn't necessarily have to conform to your individual beliefs, but that's the way I've worked it out in my mind. For several years after my diagnosis, I was told by acquaintances and friends how very strong I am to face this diagnosis. I never fully understood this reaction. Why were people telling me I was brave? Or strong? Or even admirable? What was I supposed to do once I had been given this diagnosis? The way I see it, I had no choice, but to continue my life as always. Sure, I could have plunged into a deep depression and hidden away from the world, but anybody that knows me knows that I simply can't do that. Although I may have not been aware of it at the time, I was "grabbing the bull by the horns" so to speak, and living my life.

No cure has been found for MS as of yet, but many new drugs have been developed to help patients as they deal with the daily ramifications of living with Multiple Sclerosis. There were no medications available to me when I was first diagnosed, but now there are at least a dozen medications that have been developed that help to shorten the length and duration of exacerbations in patients with MS.

Research has been shown that the earlier a patient begins these medications after being diagnosed, the less chance that person has of being permanently disabled. Now, as someone that has had more than one form of MS due to the many factors that often affect the progression of the disease, this statement is very important to anyone who is newly diagnosed. These medications, which involved from giving myself injections of manufactured medicines anywhere from every day to every other day, to once a week depending on the medication.

Finally, in 2013 my neurologist prescribed a new medication, the first oral medication was developed for Multiple Sclerosis. It is so nice not to have multiple bruises on my arms, legs, stomach, and hips from self-injecting anymore. Tecfidera has its side effects, but none nearly as miserable as being constantly bruised from the injections I was subjecting my body to on an almost-daily basis for years.

The bruising was a minor side effect of the injections. I would also experience feelings of nausea, headaches, flushing of my entire body as well as a low-grade fever within two hours of receiving each injection. I suffered through each of these side effects because I held out the hope that each medication would be THE medication to help me.

Each of these medications seemed to help control my MS by lessening the number of exacerbations I would have, but unfortunately no medicine has been developed yet to eradicate MS from the daily lives of the nearly 350,000 of persons affected by this disease in the United States alone. I would be thrilled if the scientists involved in research could develop a vaccination for MS that could be given to children after their birth. This is what I pray for now. (That, and world peace!)

I was first diagnosed with Relapsing Remitting Multiple Sclerosis, which means that the patient recovers from each exacerbation almost completely each time a relapse occurs. In fact, my first neurologist told me that he couldn't give me a positive diagnosis of MS until I'd experienced two or more exacerbations. So now I resigned myself to sitting and waiting for the next exacerbation, kind of.

I returned to my job in Dallas with the constant nagging sensation in the back of my mind that any limb in my body might be the next to go numb. Each morning I wake and begin testing my extremities, in a sort of neurological self-test I go through routinely to reassure myself that my MS hasn't progressed during the night. I start each day by wiggling my toes, flexing my ankles, bending my knees, and so forth all the way to my head. This type of self-analysis helps me to wake slowly, as well as do a little light stretching before I began each day.

It wasn't until months later when I was shopping with a friend at Neiman-Marcus in a local mall that I experienced the next set of MS symptoms. Only I didn't recognize them as symptoms of my MS. I remember that it was summer, and very hot outdoors. We were at the checkout counter of the ladies' active wear section.

Because it was summer, I had worn shorts to go shopping and I was leaning against the counter as Kelly checked out with her purchases. I recall getting impatient with her because she couldn't decide which color of shirt her sister would like more. As I tiredly leaned against the counter, my thighs brushed against the cool counter. Or maybe I should say that my left thigh was touching the coolness of the counter, while my right thigh rested on a decidedly hot counter! I stood there, quietly taking in the sensations while the clerk finished Kelly's purchase.

Upon getting her receipt, Kelly turned away and began walking towards the exit. As Kelly began to walk away, I called her back to the counter and asked her to feel the side of the counter where I had been standing. She dutifully touched the side of the counter and reported as it being cool to her touch. That's what I was afraid she would say. This must be the dreaded second exacerbation of MS that I had feared would come. Kelly dropped me off at my apartment then, and you can imagine what I did next; sleep! We had planned on catching a matinee showing of the popular movie Top Gun, but my health came first.

The holidays came around as usual. It was my first

holiday season without a Significant Other in my life. I managed quite well, if I say so myself. It was difficult, but not unbearable. I flew home to spend Christmas Day with my family, and flew back to Dallas 3 days later.

My friends in Dallas threw a surprise birthday party for me the same night that I flew in from Arkansas, which helped soften the post-holiday let-down. I returned to work the following Monday, and of course we spent our lunch hour planning another Spring Break trip. We were going to spend the week in Cancun, Mexico.

We knew that we were beyond typical college ages, but we were still young enough to enjoy the college-aged antics that we had enjoyed while in school. We planned a trip for the third week in March. I was already excited for it. Each of us cleared the time off from work with our bosses, and began planning our week of fun in the sun.

The remainder of the winter passed uneventfully with my friends and I anxiously preparing for our trip to Cancun and awaiting spring to arrive. It couldn't come quickly enough, and several of the girls in the group started going to tanning beds after Valentine's Day to get started on a base tan for our week in Mexico. I have never been in a tanning bed in my life, and I wasn't about to start now. I would just be the pale person in our group, but no way was I going to pay good money to sit in a metal "tomb" while being flooded with manufactured light rays that I am sure cause skin cancer. I will get my wrinkles naturally, thank you very much!

Around mid-February, my MS decided my life was going too well for me and chose to make itself known to me once again. I had managed to securely place my diagnosis in the back of my mind, and as a result was not taking care of myself like I should be dong. No, I wasn't into illegal drugs, but my "drug" of choice was staying up until the early morning hours on multiple occasions. That was as bad for me as any illegal drug would have been, because MS is truly a fatiguing disease, first and foremost. I began needing a lot more sleep than I was willing for my body to take, and that fact alone caused another exacerbation to come along.

This time it wasn't a major exacerbation, but it was enough for me to retreat once again to Arkansas to rest and recover for a week or two. It was one day while recovering at my childhood home that I got the shock of my life. Well, one of them anyway. The phone at my parent's house rang, and upon answering it, I was surprised to hear my bosses' voice. Mr. Ross spent several minutes inquiring as to my health, and justifiably so. The next thing I knew, Mr. Ross was saying,

"I'm sorry, Nancy, but we no longer need you at work."
WHAT???

The truth was that I *didn't* understand, and simply held the phone to my ear in shock. Half of me was telling myself that he is playing a joke on me, as I could hear some of my co-workers in the background. I said as much to mom as I was placing the phone in the cradle.

"I'm sure he will call back, and tell me it was all a joke," I told mom, who was standing beside the bed, listening to my end of conversation. "He will, won't he mom?" I heard my voice tremble unwillingly as I slowly came to the realization.

"I'm sorry, Nancy," she said while turning toward the

door. "I really don't think he will, honey; I think you were just fired." She attempted to give me a hug then, but I was simply sitting on the bed unresponsively.

I sat on the bed willing the phone to ring again with news that it was a joke, but that call never came. That was it, my life and friends in Dallas were over. No more lunches with friends, no trip to Cancun, there would be no more Happy Hours at our favorite bar, no more less-than-adequate softball games and practices, no more of anything that had made my life what it was-- fun, friends, and filled with memories. At least no one could take the memories away from me.

The news slowed my recovery from the latest exacerbation somewhat, and it added more stress for sure. It was about three weeks until I felt strong enough to make the trip to Dallas for the final time. Dad, mom, and I made the trip one weekend in March to empty my apartment of all the clothes, books, and furniture I had accumulated... and all my dead houseplants! It was difficult for me to be moving out of my apartment on the same weekend I had planned a trip to Cancun just 6 months before. A depression set in.

I settled back into my childhood bedroom at my parent's house. I recall one morning sitting in bed, trying to plan my day; would I nap before or after Jeopardy! That's the only game show that I watch almost religiously, and depending on the questions, I felt really smart after watching the thirty-minute program, or more often than not I was faced with how much I *didn't* know! Sadly, it was the highlight of my day, most days.

Yes, I was a college graduate who had been fired from

a very nice job in Dallas, and was unable to find a job locally. I became adjusted to a routine of sleeping and watching television while my parents worked each day at their office in town. I collected Unemployment for the maximum length of time allowed, while putting a resume together and checking the local newspaper for jobs... I wasn't picky, but I didn't want to flip burgers with my college degree! I can honestly say now that I thought I was too good to work a minimum wage job, so I decided more education would be the best way of occupying my days. I enrolled at one of the local universities in town, and decided that Speech Pathology would be an interesting choice for a career.

For the next few years, I would reside in my hometown. My parents bought a small house a block from our church to have as a rental income. I lived there rent free for a few years, going back to school for a Master's degree. Let me say at this point that a huge support group be it family, friends or whatever, is the key to making one's life tolerable or manageable. At least it is for me. My parents and family's support during difficult times with MS has made an enormous impact on my ability to overcome the many hurdles that are associated with MS.

I attended classes at both universities in town, and was excited about beginning a new career as a Speech-Language Pathologist. Carol enjoyed it, and I guess I received an interest in it by osmosis! I did enjoy going back to school, and just needed a few of the basic courses that would help me get into graduate school. I would spend the next two and a half years taking classes part time, just a few classes per semester.

One day, a job in Little Rock caught my eye as I was reading the paper. It was a position for an Instruction Writer with a company that published craft magazines, pamphlets, and books. After an initial interview, I was given an assignment to develop an advertising campaign for the company's annual cross-stitch calendar, and asked to bring it back to them the next day, as well as some samples of my work.

I diligently worked on that assignment as soon as I arrived home, as well as collected various samples of my cross-stitching and craft projects to take to them. I had been an avid crafter of cross-stitch designs since childhood, so finding samples of my workmanship was easy. Deciding which to show them was much more difficult. Some of my favorite projects had been made for friends and family as gifts and were unavailable for me to show Leisure-Thyme Arts.

The editors at Leisure-Thyme Arts were impressed with what I managed to assemble, and I was told the next day that I would be hired. I lived with my aunt and uncle in Little Rock for a few weeks until I found an apartment. I couldn't wait to move into my own apartment. My life was gradually taking shape once again.

After my promising job in Dallas, and the subsequent loss of that job, I was anxious to begin my life as a single, professional woman once again. Things were looking up, and I was managing my MS quite well. Nothing was going to stop me, not even a diagnosis of MS! I am determined to overcome this disease, and I am also stubborn enough to believe that I can do it.

If I stay out of the direct sunlight for any length

of time, and remain indoors with the air conditioner blasting cool air, I am fine. This is because sunlight, saps the strength from my body, as does the humidity. If I wish to remain outdoors in the heat and humidity, I must first take precautions by packing ice packs into pockets, behind my neck, at my wrists and ankles, etc. I learned this after several years of becoming over heated and nearly collapsing.

I have a large, bulky fisherman's-type vest that I wear over my clothes that has multiple pockets for the ice packs. I have learned that MS is a disease whose symptoms worsen in heat. Most MS patients are adversely affected by heat and humidity, and I am no different. Heat and humidity are two things Arkansas is known to have in abundance each summer.

I have since learned that this is not necessarily the case for all people diagnosed with MS. There are many people living with MS who find the warmth of the sun relaxing to their MS symptoms, and the high levels of humidity which affect my mobility are not a major factor in their lives. From what I have read, these people are in the minority. I was first diagnosed with Relapsing Remitting Multiple Sclerosis which means that the patient recovers from each exacerbation almost completely each time a relapse occurs.

MS has 5 levels as it progresses. Patients do not necessarily progress through all of the stages in their lifetimes. First, like many people, I was diagnosed with Relapsing-Remitting Multiple Sclerosis (RRMS). Around 85% of the people diagnosed with MS begin in this way, which means they typically are diagnosed with MS in their early 20's.

After the first diagnosis, the patient will experience symptoms that vary from mild numbness and tingling to complete loss of muscle control over the specific part of their body that is controlled by their Central Nervous System where lesions, or plaques have formed over the brain or spinal cord. This varies widely for each individual.

Eventually, most people with Relapsing Remitting MS (RRMS) will progress to Secondary Progressive MS (SPMS). This is my diagnosis, and this is where my MS is holding for the moment. I have not had a major exacerbation in several years, and I attribute this to being aware of when I need rest, and taking care of myself.

After living with relapsing-remitting MS for many years, most people will get secondary progressive MS. In this type, symptoms begin a steady march without relapses or remissions. (In this way, it's like primary progressive MS.) The change typically happens between 10 and 20 years after you're diagnosed with relapsing-remitting MS. (What Are the Different Types of Multiple Sclerosis?).

There is a slow decline in how well my nerves and muscles work, which affects the ability to move my arms and legs as I was once able to do, and my muscle movements will become more difficult harder as my MS progresses.

If there is one thing that I have learned from my years of having MS, it's that you really can't plan on things happening a certain way for yourself. Life is that way, as is living with a diagnosis of MS. It reminds me of a Jewish saying, how can you make God laugh? Simply tell him your plans! It makes me smile to think that God would listen to us make our plans, then allow Life to happen to us as it does! God already knows where our lives will take us. It is up to us to do something good with our lives.

I guess I sound like some sort of Pollyanna when I mention if life gives you lemons, make lemonade! I happen to think that's an important value by which to live, no matter your circumstances. I've been trying my hardest to make some of the most excellent lemonade for 31 years now.

Works Cited:

What Are the Different Types of Multiple Sclerosis? 2017. Electronic. 23 May 2017.

IS CHIVALRY DEAD?

D o you ever wonder how your life might be different, were it not for any particular circumstances? I do. In fact, it was my clumsiness in 1991 that eventually led to me living in the country with my husband, two daughters, three dogs and a cat, and my parents as neighbors. It is very likely that none of the aforementioned facts would have happened, had I not fallen in 1991. The fact that I fell very ungracefully while walking down a steep hill toward church one January morning can be held responsible, in one way or another, for the way my life has turned out.

It is at this point that I should tell you that I was single then, and lived in a city that is much larger than my hometown of 10,000. Although the city was populated by 200,000 fellow Arkansans, I had found a church home that made me feel as though I was among dear friends.

On this particular Sunday, I parked my car; spoke to a woman whom I had befriended recently, and hurried off to what I knew would be a warm sanctuary for services. Jan stopped me, to introduce her adult son to me, and after a perfunctory handshake, the three of us hurried down the steep hill to the church.

It was at this precise moment that my right foot slipped on a patch of ice that had escaped the shovels the hardworking men of the church who cleared the parking lot each Sunday morning before services began. I didn't even see the ice before my foot landed on it, wearing a brand-new pair of black patent leather pumps that I had bought the day before at a local mall. I had worn them this day, thinking I would break the stiffness out of the shoes by wearing them to church. I knew it would be far easier to slip my shoes off during the sermon than to slip them off my feet while at work. One moment I was shaking hands with Jan's son, and the next moment I was flat on my back on the frozen ground, looking up at both Jan and her son, who were bent over me with concern.

I should mention that Jan was showing concern for my well-being, and her son was rather red in the face, attempting (but definitely failing) to stifle his laughter. When I tell this story, many people act in a very shocked manner almost to the point of disgust in his seemingly immature reaction to my unfortunate fall.

However, Steve has taught me that one of the most important things about dealing with the challenges of a disease such as MS is that it is important to have a sense of humor with what often seem like the most difficult times in life. The saying that: "The only thing I could do was laugh instead of crying" can be so true.

As Jan's son held his hand out to help me to my feet, I brushed it away, refusing to give him the satisfaction of assisting me from my very unladylike position on the frozen ground, as well as allowing him to laugh at my predicament. The three of us went into the church, and then to our respective classes for fellowship, coffee, doughnuts, and Sunday school, which I was secretly hoping would shame Jan's son into an apology for laughing at me so shamelessly. Not very Christian-like, but a lady's pride had been hurt!

I limped from the sanctuary to my classroom, which entailed three sets of stairs, as well as a lengthy walk down a hallway to our room. I spent most of the time explaining my ripped pantyhose, scraped knee, and broken shoe to the flood of people passing me on the stairway. They were well-meaning of course, and the questions helped me to suppress most of my anger and embarrassment over the entire incident. As I limped my way into the classroom, our class leader was introducing a new member to the class,

"This is Steve," Lesley was saying, "he just moved to town this weekend."

At that moment, I glanced up from my lap, where I was holding my broken shoe, to see this new classmate looking directly at me. The new classmate and Jan's son, who had been laughing at me mercilessly just an hour before, were one and the same. I was mortified!

My plans to relate the morning's occurrences to a hopefully sympathetic class never came to light, and I just brushed off the fall as something that had happened on my way to church this morning, down-playing my injuries, and hoping that the newcomer could hold his tongue and keep from laughing. Much to my surprise, he didn't burst into laughter in class that day, and inquired quite honestly as to my injuries after class. He seemed nice enough, so when he asked me if I would like to go to lunch after church, I accepted.

We got to know one another a little bit over lunch. It turns out that he had moved to Little Rock the previous day. He has been living in Austin, Texas and has just gone through a bitter divorce, with accusations of adultery being thrown around by both sides. He assured me that the accusations by his ex-wife were completely unfounded, something is mother would reiterate to me months later.

Steve had been hospitalized because of bleeding ulcers and had lost a lot of weight. His mom had gone to visit him, and insisted that he move with her to Little Rock. He acquiesced, and made the move upon his release from the hospital. In Austin, he was employed with Bridgestone-Firestone as a Master auto mechanic, so he just made the transfer to one of the Little Rock branches.

We spent the next ten months getting to know one another better. We went to a lot of movies together, and I discovered that he has an amazing ability to recall facts about movies and actual movie lines word-for-word. This is not a talent according to my sister Carol, but rather something on which she prefers "not to waste her brain cells." When she first said this to him, he didn't quite know how to take it. Steve, being the good sport that he is, just followed along with the laughter that erupted from around the dinner table.

Fast forward 10 months, and Steve, Jan, and I were in church once again. This time it was the church in my hometown, and the occasion was a wedding. Our wedding.

I'll never forget my shock at seeing how empty the

church was that night as I stood in the narthex, on my father's arm as he prepared to give me away. The wedding was not anything like what I had imagined it would be in all my adolescent dreams.

I was walking down the aisle in a rented wedding dress of all things! I chose to rent a dress rather than have my parents spring for a new dress, for two main reasons. First, I had waited until it was almost too late to have a dress altered at a traditional bridal shop. Secondly, I always was in the process of losing weight, or at least trying to lose it. I didn't want a large size wedding dress hanging in my closet for the rest of my life. I just knew that my daughters, if I were to have any, would be a much smaller size than I was at the moment of their weddings!

So, here I am, walking down the aisle in a train-less and rented wedding dress, in an almost empty church, about to marry the man I had literally fallen for! The wedding was small, yet very effective. We have now been married for 25 years, and although we have had our bumpy times in the past, and are sure to have more in the future, we are in it for the long haul.

We honeymooned in a cabin in the Ozarks of northwest Arkansas for a total of four days. The trees in the Ozarks were putting forth a multitude of seasonal foliage. As it so happened, we both succumbed to allergies after the wedding, so we were not in the mood for many honeymoon activities. We woke with fevers, headaches, coughs, and every other symptom you always hear about on TV commercials in the winter. By the time we made it back to our apartment in Little Rock, we both had full-fledged sinus infections! There is nothing like starting a marriage in a sick bed, and we nursed one another back to health within a few days.

Our brief courtship and subsequent 26 years of marriage have been filled with laughter and tears, but mostly the kind that roll down your cheeks when laughing too hard. Our families think the story of our meeting, complete with my ungraceful fall, is priceless. "Nancy's Big Slip" was the topic of many familial conversations that year! Steve loves to refer to this moment as the day that "I fell for him!" and so I let him have his little moments, because later when he tried to adapt to country life I would have mine!

I also learned that I was colorblind within a year of working at Leisure-Thyme Arts and Stitching. I kept making mistakes when I was asked to inspect the finished projects before they were to be photographed for a magazine or pamphlet. I didn't think much about it, and blamed the lighting, a headache, etc. for my increasing errors.

I made an appointment for my annual ophthalmologists' check-up. Imagine my shock when he told me that I am colorblind! I'd had no idea that I was colorblind, it makes me wonder how many questionable color combinations I had worn in my lifetime? The possibilities are endless! My dad has always been colorblind, and it is a joke among the family. I never thought that I could be the focus of the lighthearted jokes, also!

Steve and I were married on November 9, 1991. Because we had inadvertently planned the wedding on the first day of deer season, as well as the date of one of the local universities' Homecoming, and also the fact that a pillar of our community had suddenly passed away the night before, which sent shockwaves through the town all contributed to our wedding not being well attended.

I'll never forget my shock at seeing how empty the church was that night as I stood in the narthex, on my father's arm as he prepared to give me away. The wedding was not anything like what I had imagined it would be in all my adolescent dreams. I mean, I was walking down the aisle in a rented wedding dress of all things!

I chose to rent a dress rather than have my parents spring for a new dress, for two main reasons. First, I had waited until it was almost too late to have a dress altered at traditional bridal shop. Secondly, I always was in the process of losing weight, or at least trying to lose it. I didn't want a large size wedding dress hanging in my closet for the rest of my life. I just knew that my daughters, if I were to have any, would be a much smaller size than I was when they decided to marry. So, here I am, walking down the aisle in a train-less wedding dress, in an almost empty church, about to marry the man I had literally fallen for!

The wedding was small, yet very effective. We have now been married for 26 years, and although we have had our bumpy times in the past, and are sure to have more in the future, we are in it for the long haul.

We honeymooned in a cabin in the Ozarks of northwest Arkansas for a total of four days. The trees in the Ozarks were putting forth a multitude of seasonal foliage. As it so happened, we both succumbed to allergies immediately after the wedding, so we were not in the mood for many honeymoon activities. We woke with fevers, headaches, coughs, and every other symptom you always hear about on TV commercials in the winter. By the time we made it back to our apartment in Little Rock, we both had full-fledged sinus infections! There is nothing like starting a marriage in a sick bed, and we nursed one another back to health within a few days.

Eventually we got over our sinus infections, and life returned to normal for us as newlyweds. I had started a new job as a Chiropractic Assistant right before our wedding. I never seemed to shake the remnants of the honeymoon illness, and began feeling nauseous each day around meal times. On a lark, I did what a colleague suggested and took a pregnancy test. I knew I couldn't be pregnant because I took a birth control pill each day like clockwork, so I sent my urine to be tested at the lab the clinic used for all other procedures.

The next day was an unusually busy one at the clinic and the results of my pregnancy test were the last thing on my mind. I was standing at the front desk when the messenger from the lab brought in the previous days' lab results. Like I said, it was an unusually busy day at the clinic, so I just reached across the counter and got the stack of results and placed them in the towering IN box for the secretary to file later. I noticed that the messenger stood around longer than usual, with a huge smile on her face, but was so busy I didn't think twice about it. I hurried off to my next patient and didn't come back to the front for over two hours.

When I did get a chance to catch my breath, I sat down to help file the lab results into the corresponding charts. Guess who's was right on top?? I glanced at the sheet on the top and saw my name printed in bold letters, and beside it was the word, POSITIVE. I nearly fainted! Steve and I had discussed starting a family someday, but not for a few years. This changed things for us to be sure, but we were both excited beyond belief.

I left the clinic for long enough to drive down the street to Steve's work. I didn't say anything to him but simply held the lab results out for him to see for himself. His eyes widened as he realized what I was showing him, followed by a huge smile that spread across his face. We kissed, and then hugged, and I was on my way back to work, finding it impossible to get the goofy grin off my face. That night we finally had the time to talk about the pregnancy, the fact that the only health insurance I had was Medicare because of my MS, as well as the fact that we hadn't discussed with my neurologist that we wanted to start a family. When we met with my neurologist and shared the news, it was received with cautionary congratulations from her. She told us not to expect too much from my first pregnancy, but to try my best not to gain too much weight.

My first pregnancy was a pleasant one for me. I only gained 18 pounds, total, and because I'm so tall, most of the baby was growing vertically, instead of outwardly! My due date was December 24. I wasn't thrilled with the projected holiday birth date, but it couldn't be helped. I felt great during my pregnancy. I had always heard of pregnant women craving thing like ice cream, chocolate, and any number of non-healthy foods. In fact, I was kind of looking forward to this time of my life. How could anyone deny a pregnant woman her cravings? Just my luck, this baby made me turn down all sweets in exchange for salads! I couldn't believe it. Can't I get a break just once in my life? The one time that sweets are not entirely off limits to me, I crave salads!!

My pregnancy was uneventful for the most part. I continued working until my blood pressure spiked, but my OB/GYN didn't put me on bed rest. He just told me to take it easy the final three weeks before the due date, and to keep eating those salads! We spent Christmas Eve and Christmas Day in Arkadelphia that year, anxiously awaiting the birth of our first child. And waiting. And waiting. And waiting, for 10 days!

On January 4, 1993, we welcomed Hunter Ann Wayland into this world. And for a first-time mom, I couldn't have been happier. After being induced with Pitocin at around noon of that day, my labor moved along rather quickly. I only remember the doctor telling me to push 4 times that day, after less than an hour of hard labor. She was beautiful! At 8 lbs., 4 oz., and at 22" long she was just perfect in every way.

She was delivered quickly, so her head had not spent much time in the birth canal. She had long fingers, and a perfect, round face with the most beautiful set of lips I had ever seen! We named her Hunter as homage to my mother's side of the family and Ann was from my middle name. We had found out that I was expecting a girl months before, but I so wanted to honor my mom's parents in some way, and Steve said he could live with a masculine name for a girl, couldn't I? Shortly after her birth, I was watching television and the beautiful actress Hunter Tylo was a guest on the show I was watching. I never doubted naming our firstborn such a masculine name again.

My recovery from childbirth was quick, until my MS raised its ugly head again and reminded me that I was not like other mothers. I needed rest, and a lot of it, to keep up with an active toddler. Several times during Hunter's first 4 years I had exacerbations, but with the help of steroids, and managing my energy as best I could, I succeeded in prevailing over my MS for the most part.

The number one rule that I tell any first-time mother is to sleep when your baby sleeps. I did this religiously until my daughters began kindergarten…and even a few years beyond! My life before MS didn't leave time for napping, and my health paid for it. I'm not saying that everyone needs a 3-hour deep sleep in the middle of the day, but I am always amazed at how revitalized I feel even after a 15-minute break.

Hunter has grown into the most amazing 22-year old graduate student that I know! She is currently working towards a Master's degree in Environmental Toxicology at a school only an hour away. She definitely got her brains from her father. Hunter went to college after high school on a very impressive scholarship. She has always been mature beyond her years, and as a child it was hard work getting her to smile, she kept such a serious expression on her face at all times!

Her sister is equally as talented and smart as our first-born. I used to remark how very different their personalities were from one another when they were younger. It was almost as though we were raising two entirely separate individuals at times. Hunter was more serious, while Sloan always seems to have a bright smile for whoever is lucky enough to be the recipient. They both are kind, caring individuals with wonderful senses of humor. They almost need be this way, given that Steve and I are their parents!

I'll never forget the night Steve and I told Hunter she would be getting a little brother or sister. We were sitting in a booth inside Red Lobster and I leaned over the table and said,

"Guess what, Hunter? God has chosen you to be a big sister for the baby we're going to have this summer!"

She jumped out of the booth, ran to my side, and hugged my neck as though her life depended on it. "Thank you, mommy, thank you, thank you," she kept repeating over and over.

She had been asking why her friends had babies at their homes, but we didn't have one at our house. We had told her that if it was right for us to be parents again, that God would make it happen. Honestly, Steve and I had been debating it among ourselves.

We knew the potential for my MS to get much worse if I were to have a second child. Of course, no one could tell us the percentages, or any other statistics. We decided to let God lead in the way our family should go, and He answered us by giving me another wonderful pregnancy and a second, beautiful daughter four years after our first.

My second pregnancy was a breeze! I felt great throughout, but this time I didn't crave salads! Yes, unfortunately my cravings were leaning more towards Taco Bell, French fries of any sort, and chocolate! Amazingly, I didn't indulge these cravings very often and I gained an even 20 pounds with the second pregnancy.

I did pretty much the same things as I did the first

time; walking, resting, and preparing myself mentally for the birth. Once again, the baby was late, by almost 2 full weeks. I guess that I provided such a good home for them while they were still inside me, neither of them was in a rush to leave! One thing that made this pregnancy worse was the fact that I was pregnant in the summer. Summertime, Arkansas, and MS did not go well together that year. It seemed much hotter than normal, as well as more humid!! It may have been the fact that I was pregnant.

We had decided not to find out the sex of this baby, so it was a surprise in the delivery room to hear, "It's a girl!"

My mother in law was present once again for the birth, and she told me that I said, "Oh, another one!" before I laid my head down on the pillow.

It's not that I was disappointed, because I wasn't. As a child, growing up the third of three daughters, I always assumed that my children would be boys. I don't know why I thought that, but I did.

Even the dolls that I had as a child were named boy names, except for my favorite doll that I received one Christmas, whom I named Dorothy once my younger cousin was born the following May. I used to cut her hair repeatedly until she had no more to cut. Dorothy was the most beautiful bald baby doll I could ever imagine. Beauty is in the eyes of the beholder, after all!

Mom recently found my beloved Dorothy while cleaning out her house in preparation for downsizing. Dorothy now sits proudly in my bedroom, but my daughters insist that she is creepy! I tell them that beauty is all in the eyes of the beholder, to which they scoff and walk away.

Lily Sloan was born on July 24, 1997, was 23" long, weighed 8 pounds, 6 ounces and was just gorgeous! My labor and delivery was just as quick as it had been with Hunter, so she also didn't have the typical newborn "cone head" either, which was fine with us! We named her Lily, after my great grandmother, and also Steve's great-grandmother. Sloan was the name of one of my great aunts on my mom's side of the family.

At the time, my speech was a little slurred from my MS, and I couldn't pronounce Lily to save my life, so she has always gone by the name of Sloan. She was the second-most beautiful baby I had ever seen! Her lashes looked like butterflies resting on her eyelids they were so long, and she just glows. She, like her sister, didn't have much hair to start off with, but they both had thick beautiful hair by the time they started school. I think it's neat how our kids have such strong family names. Once when we were flying to Albuquerque to visit Steve's family, Sloan came out of the airport restroom and said accusingly,

"Now I know the real story of where you came up with my name!" Steve and I looked at her, not understanding where the conversation was heading, when she further clarified her statement.

"The toilets all have my name on them!" It seems a company named Sloane is the manufacturer of plumbing equipment and supplies. She will not let us forget that to this day…Ah, kids.

The only thing I can say about having children is that it is a personal decision for everybody. Would we have not had children if we had known it would hurry my days in a wheelchair? I don't think anything would change. We prayed to God to bless us with another child or not, and I am thankful each day that He did. My children have brought us so much joy and happiness I don't even want to think what my life would be like without them!

Embracing the Differences in City Life versus Country Life

Many times in our marriage the differences in our backgrounds have come to the surface. Even the names we each called our grandparents are different from one another. Steve grew up calling his grandparents Grandma and Grandpa. Both sets of grandparents! The names for my grandparents were a little more original, my mom's parents were Ma'am-ma and Daddy-pa. My father's parents were Granny and Papa, and I can say with assurance that none of the multitude of grandchildren ever confused one grandparent for another! To this day, if Steve is relaying some past event that happens to include his grandparents, I always find myself asking to which grandparent he is referring in his story!

There have come about many other differences in our backgrounds. One of which was where we got firewood for the fireplace. Since I was raised in the country, my idea of collecting firewood involved going into the woods to cut up fallen trees and hauling them back to the house to stack and use all winter. Now I'll be the first to admit that it is my dad doing all the work, but I would help unload the firewood once he brought it to the house, if I couldn't find a way out of helping with this chore. Steve's idea of getting firewood involved driving to the nearest 7-11 convenience store to get firewood that has been neatly packaged into overpriced bundles for purchase.

The same can be said for our Christmas tree. My family would make a day of searching the woods for the perfect tree, chopping it down, and bringing it home while singing Christmas carols at the top of our lungs. Steve's family would go down the street to the nearest tree lot to buy their tree, and hopefully they would get it home before all the needles fell off!

I'm not saying that my family's way of doing things is better than Steve's family's- I am just pointing out the differences in our upbringings. I grew up on a cattle farm, where my grandfather and father tended to a large herd of cattle. As a country girl, I knew that each Saturday morning would involve working at the farm, herding cattle for one reason or another. With my cousins, I would help separate the cows and calves for vaccination, help tag the cows, tag the calves, move them to another pasture, and even help round all the little bull calves for castration purposes. That last chore always made me feel a little guilty, and I felt sorry for them as they cried out in pain when their male parts were taken from them.

I tell you this because before we were married, Steve rode along with my dad to look for a loose cow that had broken through a fence and was headed toward a neighbor's pond. In his effort to make conversation with my dad, Steve boldly made the comment,

"Mr. Wasson, you sure do have a lot of bulls in your herd."

To which my dad replied, "No, I just have the one!" Steve sat quietly for several minutes, wondering where he had gone wrong.

"The ones with horns are all females," my father told him, leaving Steve to ponder that fact for a while in silence. That silence is followed by my father and me both biting our tongues very hard to keep from bursting out in laughter. This may have been the first time for these memorable and comical moments but it would also not be the last.

Dad held his laughter until we got home, when dad told Steve to tell the family what he said about the number of bulls in our herd. It seems the city boy thought that horns made the bulls, and not the anatomy! We still laugh over that, as well as the time dad told Steve that the cow trails meandering throughout the pastures, 4-inch wide paths in the fields that were void of grass growing in them, were actually snake trails and he should be on the look-out for the monstrous snakes that make the trails. I can only imagine what must have going through his mind, picturing massive anaconda-esque snakes wandering the pastures of southwest Arkansas! Steve learned early in our relationship to not take anything my dad says too seriously.

I learned Steve had truly acclimated to my family when our oldest daughter was in second grade and he told her that the photo in the new frame of the African American child was her half-sister, and she would be moving in with us soon. She got very excited, and it was heartbreaking to tell her that the picture was just a stock photo from the company that makes the frame. We never knew that she wanted a sister so badly. She promptly forgot ever wanting a sister and denies to this day that she doesn't remember begging for one!

It wasn't long before Steve joined in the revelry and tried to trick members of my family into believing some of his tall tales. For example, one evening as we were all sitting outside around a campfire, Steve had my entire family believing him when he told us that it was a night much like this one, when he had taken his dog for a late-night stroll on the golf course across the street from his family's home in Albuquerque and he had witnessed a UFO landing on the golf course.

My entire family jumped in with questions for him, not doubting his sincerity one bit. I knew he would fit right into my crazy family when he burst out with a huge laugh, after answering several questions with a straight face!

CHILDREN: THE RIPPLES
THAT BECAME A TSUNAMI

I generally follow my doctor's advice on things, especially when it comes to factors regarding my MS. However, when my first neurologist told me it would be best for me not to have children; I knew that one day I *would* have children! I don't think anyone should have the power to decide for you if reproduction is in the cards. When my first neurologist, Dr. Gaines, gave me his recommendation, I accepted it. After all, I wasn't married yet and having babies was not even on the radar for me!

When Steve and I married in November 1991, we practiced birth control in the form of birth control pills. However, I was adamant (at least to myself) about being a parent. I had spent my childhood being a mommy to a wide assortment of dolls, and had always pictured having children. I'm pretty sure my parents never pictured my life without children. By this time, I was already the proud aunt to 2 nieces and 3 nephews. Steve has a niece and 3 nephews, and I unashamedly called them mine as well.

Our families have continued to grow in the past 25

years, and we now claim 6 nieces and nephews on the Wasson side of the family, and 8 on the Wayland side. We also are proud great-aunt-and-uncle to 10 great-nieces and great-nephews! Yes, our families have grown quite a bit, and will continue to grow. Family. That is what life is all about, or should be anyway.

I began feeling more lethargic than usual during the cold winter months of 1992. I was working as a Chiropractic Assistant in downtown Little Rock. I enjoyed the job, it gave me plenty of opportunities to use my interpersonal skills with both doctors and patients. It was not a salaried position, but I loved it!

The clinic was small, but large in the number of patients it served. I worked from 7:30-5:00 most days. I was on my feet most of the time while at work. In March, I began feeling sick. I munched on saltine crackers by the handfuls to keep the almost constant nausea at bay. This lasted for a little over three months.

One of my co-workers suggested I should take a pregnancy test. I laughed because I knew I wasn't pregnant, but I sent a sample of my urine off to the lab to be tested. Any lab tests performed on employees of the clinic were free, so why not?

The next day, an employee of the lab brought the results in. We were especially busy that day, so I just grabbed the stack of papers from the messenger and shoved them into an already bursting IN box, then I went about my regular duties. I had forgotten that my results were most likely in that stack of papers.

At around three o'clock, I finally found the time to file the lab results and noticed my pregnancy test results:

POSITIVE! I was shocked, and nearly fainted right there in the office. After telling my coworkers the news, I asked the office manager if I could take a late lunch break to tell Steve the good news in person. I hurriedly drove to Steve's work, and without saying anything, simply showed him the lab result.

It took him several moments to comprehend what he was looking at, but when he did, a huge smile came across his face. That was all I needed from him, his smile said loads to me, and I returned to work feeling at peace. I had no idea how my MS would be affected by pregnancy, but I was sure we could handle it. It meant starting a family a few years earlier than we had planned, but it was happening.

As it turned out, my MS went into remission for the length of my pregnancy. In fact, I had never felt better! It seems that for some people with MS, all symptoms of the disease go into remission while the body is pregnant. In fact, it made me wonder why scientists can't come up with a hormone or something that would make my body think it was pregnant all the time! But alas, science is not that simple.

On January 4, 1993 I went in for a scheduled appointment with my obstetrician. My mother in law came with me to the appointment, and I'm awfully glad she was there! It turns out that the nagging backache I had complained to Steve about all night was actually the beginning of contractions! I was dilated to 3 and a half centimeters already, but what was more disconcerting was the fact that my blood pressure was elevated immensely. This alarmed me because I had always had low blood pressure throughout my pregnancy.

My doctor told me that the baby was coming today, and I should go check in at the hospital right away. Jan and I immediately left the doctor's office and headed to Steve's work to let him know. He was working at Chevron, and his boss told him he really couldn't leave until he finished the three vehicles he was working on.

Steve came to my car and said, "I'm sorry Nan, but Tony says I've got to finish these three cars before I go. You go ahead, and I'll be there as soon as I can." Steve sounded distressed, but he really didn't think he had a choice. I was disappointed, but had known this was a possibility. My mother in law got out of my car and immediately walked up to Steve's manager,

"Tony, I don't think you understand. Nancy is having the baby, and I don't think you want her to go into full labor here in your parking lot! Steve needs to come with us right now," in a very definitive voice. Jan turned around without awaiting his reply, opened the car door, and sat down. "Now, let's get to the hospital!"

The three of us were checking into the hospital within the next 20 minutes. My labor hadn't fully started yet, and it didn't progress any once I was in the maternity ward. After a few hours, my doctor gave me a little bit of Pitocin through my IV to induce labor. My blood pressure was continuing to rise, and the doctor said it would be best for the baby to be delivered ASAP. My labor began in earnest an hour later, and just a little after 1:00 p.m. after a total of four pushes, I gave birth to the most beautiful 8 pound,

4-ounce baby girl any of us had ever seen, and we were not biased in the least bit!

We named our first-born Hunter Ann Wayland. We knew at the time that it was rather forward-thinking to name our child such a masculine first name, but I was adamant that I wanted her name to reflect a sense of family. My mom's maiden name was Hunter, and I thought that name sounded strong for either a boy or a girl.

I almost regretted giving Hunter the masculine name once, while I was shopping for groceries. Hunter was about 3 months old and I had dressed her in a pair of pink and white pinstriped overalls for our outing. To top it off, I had taped a pink bow to her head so that no one could mistake her for a boy! Going down the first aisle of the store, an elderly couple approached our cart and began oohing and aahing over how cute my son was,

"Look at that adorable little boy, Henry" I heard the woman say as I passed them. It's okay, I thought to myself, they just didn't notice Hunter's pink overalls. As I continued my shopping, two elderly women approached me, "Oh, Elizabeth," said the taller one, "Look at this precious little boy, isn't he just the cutest thing you've ever seen?" The second woman, Elizabeth, then looked at me, "How old is he? Babies are such a gift from God, don't you think?"

I was taken aback, "Yes, ma'am they certainly are!" While thinking to myself; *Can't you see that I dressed her in pink? What is going on? This is the second couple to mention my "son"! There is even a solid pink diaper bag sitting beside her!* I then spoke up that she was eleven weeks old, and that her name was Hunter Ann.

After getting some puzzled looks from the couple, I explained that Hunter was a family name. The women then told me she was beautiful, and to be sure to treasure my time with her. I thanked them and proceeded with my shopping. A few aisles later the exact same thing occurred with a group of multi-generational women. And it happened again in the check-out line as well as the parking lot! I was beginning to feel as though I was a broken recording! Needless to say, Steve and were both anxious for her to have a head full of hair, so that we could fill her hair with ribbons and bows.

I love being a stay at home mom, even though Steve's work and school schedule keep him away from home a lot. I often joked that I felt like a single mother, doing all the duties of mother and father. I would even find myself getting angry at Steve for leaving me alone with all the chores, shopping, cooking, cleaning, washing, drying, folding, paying bills, etc.

Whenever I was in this mindset, I would resent Steve's college classes as well as his work. *At least he talked to adults every day*! That's when I decided to find a day program for Hunter to attend, so I would at least have a few hours a day to myself, two days a week. I found a Children's Day Out program at a church down the street from our tiny rental house. Hunter thrived there, as did I. Some days I would leave Hunter, and later Sloan, at CDO from 9:00 until 3:00, but most days I would arrive early to hang out with the other moms on the playground.

I made some very good friends with the other moms, and their parenting styles were as different from mine as our children. It was not unusual to see Indigo, whose mom was Carla, wearing a Halloween princess costume to school in February, because, as Carla said, "She wanted to be a princess today." I learned a lot about being a mom from these women! The result being that 4-year-old Hunter ended up being in a color photograph wearing a pink and purple striped shirt with her red, yellow, and navy madras plaid shorts one day on the front page of our state-wide newspaper! She was colorful, to say the least.

Of course, she doesn't remember her insistence at wearing the colorful combination that day. I was mortified when Steve and Hunter came back to the house after collecting insects for his Biology class assignment. I'll never forget the nonchalant way that he mentioned the photographer to me, "Oh, by the way, Hunter and I might be in the paper sometime this week".

Imagine my surprise when it appeared on the front page of the state-wide newspaper the next day! One glance at the photo and all hopes of it being printed in black and white on a less prominent page went out the window. Before I had befriended Carla and the other moms in the group, I would have been embarrassed by the photo. Instead of focusing on the lack of color and pattern coordination that screamed at me, I learned to focus instead on Hunter's happiness as she helped her dad collect insects. Yes, Carla, Katrina, and Beth helped me to loosen up and enjoy my children more. This didn't mean that I gave Hunter full control over her wardrobe choices, but I was more lenient than some other moms that I knew.

I think that helped in other ways, too. For example, I was most likely to be the only mother in my kids' preschool and elementary classrooms with a walker or a wheelchair. That fact never seemed to bother my kids very much, they just accepted the fact that I was disabled. They didn't know me in any other way. I was the room mother for Hunter's kindergarten and first grade classes and went to her school weekly to read, craft, or just be another warm body in the room. I treasured those days, mainly because I realized just how much of a difference a little attention some of these kids were hungering, and what an enormous difference a weekly visit to a classroom can make. I like to think that I touched the other kids' lives, as well as my own.

Each year, toward the beginning of the school year my visit would include information on Multiple Sclerosis. I definitely didn't want my children to feel left out, or ostracized in any way simply because they had a mom that couldn't walk. I also like to think that my presence in the classrooms might have helped to lessen the amount of prejudice that these kids would grow up with. I wanted them to each see that I was normal, and could give hugs just as well from a sitting position as others can by standing.

Sometimes the students would be timid to be near me at first, but I always informed them that MS was not "catching". After they understood that, I would give and receive more hugs than I could count! The hours I spent in my daughters' classrooms were some of the most fulfilling, and almost made me wish that I had become a teacher myself. (I said almost!)

The Arkansas chapter of the National Multiple Sclerosis Society helped many times by giving me pamphlets and coloring books to take to the classes. I feel like a one-person public relations team, trying to get information to the public on the disease that I know far too well. It's not easy describing Multiple Sclerosis. There can be 100,000 people with the disease, each person experiencing different symptoms. Not just slightly different, but some differences can be quite vast.

For example, I cannot handle the heat and humidity of Arkansas summers, while some people with MS find the heat soothing to their symptoms. If I am in Arkansas during the summer, I spend the days and nights inside an air-conditioned environment. Is it any wonder that autumn is my very favorite time of the year? Spring is nice too, but the threat of 100 + degree weather, coupled with high humidity, is always on the horizon.

Autumn brings with it the promise of cooler weather as well as my favorite time of year, the holiday season. I have always loved the Christmas season, because of the sense of family and wonderment that pervades each moment this time of year.

On average, I have noticed that men with MS tend to experience the disease differently from women with MS. At least, in my experiences that has seemed the norm, but I am no scientist or doctor, so please don't quote me on that. The truth is that MS is a progressive neuro-muscular disease and there are different forms of it, and different stages within each form. When I was diagnosed 31 years ago, I had relapsing-remitting MS. This meant I did not have daily, visible symptoms but if I didn't take care of myself and whenever I overdid the activities of the singles lifestyle Dallas had to offer, I would pay for it with a numbness in some part of my body in the following days, weeks, or even months.

Then I will experience an exacerbation of my symptoms, the doctor will prescribe me bed rest and Prednisone daily until I recovered. My recovery would be minimal at first, but after about a week or so, I will awaken with no symptoms at all. I would have the side effects of the Prednisone, though. At one time, I was taking over 80mg daily just to keep my MS in check!

If you have ever taken this medication for any reason at all, you know the side effects, and believe me when I tell you I've had them all! The weight gain, the puffy face, swollen everything. Night sweats, chills, heart palpitations, jittery nerves, dry skin, scalp, and mouth. I don't remember how often I would pray for a medication to help manage exacerbations. Little did I know that such a medication was right around the corner.

The medicine was named Betaseron, and it came in the form of injections that I or someone close, would give me every other day. I attended a training session at the hospital in Little Rock and was shown how to inject the liquid in one small bottle onto the cube of medicine in another small bottle without causing bubbles, then get another syringe and draw the medicine into a sterile syringe to inject it in the designated area of my body. I was warned to always rotate the injection areas, because if I use the same area too often, it will cause hard callous-like areas to form, and I wouldn't be able to use the area again.

Surprisingly my favorite area to inject is about 1"above/below my naval. I thought at first it would hurt, but because there are so few nerves in that area, it never did, unless I didn't give the medicine time to warm to room temperature first. I was given a chart showing the areas on the body to inject, making sure to rotate the areas each day I received the injection. Then the side effects begin, and they are not easy to live with.

Mostly, the feeling of being flushed that would come over my body less than an hour after the injections was annoying. Then I would experience a fever along with muscle aches and pains that felt as though I had the flu for the rest of the night. These symptoms would then dissipate while I slept. Within 30 minutes after the injection, a bright red circular mark appears, about 3" in diameter, rising above the rest of my skin. It would present as a huge hive on my leg, arm, back, or stomach. Then the fever would follow, as well as the constant itching. The Betaseron caused me so much discomfort the nights I would take it, I only slept well on nights I didn't have an injection. That's not all, because the next day the red whelps would turn to big, ugly, bruises on my pale skin, and remain for weeks.

I just accepted the fact that I would be sporting bruises from the injections and lived my life as normally as I knew how. One day, I took Hunter swimming at the local Y and noticed an older woman looking at my bruises while Hunter and I were changing into our street clothes before leaving one day. I didn't think anything of her glances until she came to me with a handful of pamphlets about spousal abuse. Catching me off-guard, I automatically took her outstretched hand and put the pamphlets in my gym bag, telling her thank you. As she gave me a big hug, and whispered Bless You in my ear, I suddenly realized what was happening. She thought the bruises were a sign of abuse from someone, my husband? I then explained to her the reasons for all the bruises on my legs, arms, and torso, but I wasn't sure that she believed me.

Luckily my Mother in Law walked into the dressing area, and seeing the two of us hugging one another, helped me to clear the story with the concerned woman. I thank God for the woman who saw what she thought was an abused woman and reached out to me. I hope the fact that I wasn't abused didn't deter her from reaching out to others, some who may need her assistance.

I continued with the Betaseron for several more years until the medical establishment thankfully developed an oral medication, Techviderra. The side effects were the same as Betaseron's, but at least this was in large capsule form, and didn't cause bruising. Today there are numerous medications for MS, but nothing to cure it yet. Over the years, I have been on numerous drugs for MS, most were injections such as Ampyra, Aubagio, Avonex, Betaseron, Copaxone, Extavia, Gilinya, Glatopa, Lemtrada, Novantrone, Pelgridy, Rebif, Tecfidera, Tysabri, and Zinbryfa, all of which are considered disease-modifying drugs. I personally tried a handful of them with varying levels of effectiveness. Your doctor is the only one who can tell you which medicine might be best for you.

It is difficult to measure the effectiveness of these drugs because the effectiveness is measured by the lack of MS symptoms. In fact, this element alone is the one reason I was removed from the group insurance policy at Steve's place of employment. Each month, a lady from his work would call me to see how I was doing. After 9 months of doing this, and with me not reporting any improvement with my MS, Steve's employer decided the expensive medication I was injecting myself with was not working. Rather than seeing no exacerbations as a good sign, the big-wigs in their corporate offices saw it as a failure, and decided to end my coverage.

We were both shocked when this happened, because only then did we discover that the lady from the corporate office who called me each month was, in fact, a corporate "spy" who would make a report based on our conversation for the higher-ups in the organization. I felt betrayed and nauseated when we discovered this fact, and wondered to myself if I in some way had said something to her during a phone call that had precipitated the decision to drop my insurance.

We appealed the decision with signed statements from my neurologist, the MS society, and the medicine itself, but to no avail. The company refused to reinstate my insurance or pay for any more medication. As I feared, my MS came once again shortly thereafter, proving to us at least that the injections had been working.

I am constantly amazed at the number of drugs that are available to patients with MS, as there were none when I was first diagnosed in 1986. It's exciting to see just how far medicine has come in my lifetime, but I also realize that our society still has a way to go. Every day I am reminded of just how lucky I am to be alive in this day and age. Wonder is all around us if we just take the time to notice it, and most of all thank God for it every day.

The thing that gets under my skin and won't let go is the fact that the costs of these drugs are astronomical. We were a young family, and couldn't afford the $1,500.00/month + that these drugs cost. We reached out to the companies who manufacture these medications, and almost every company has a patient assistance fund. If you are willing to go through loads of paperwork, phone calls, and endless questions, as well as to wait patiently for answers, there are people in this world who can and will help you afford the medications needed.

Currently, I am not taking any specific medication for my MS, and that is approved by my neurologist. I still see him on regular basis, every 6 months, and he has me taking antidepressants and muscle relaxers on a daily basis to help me cope with depression, and muscle tightness in my legs especially, plus an OTC multi vitamin Supplement, and an extra 400 IU of Vitamin D daily, but that's about it. I try to eat healthy meals most of the time, as well as use exercise bands to help build/maintain muscle in my arms.

Having MS for 31 years has definitely caused my life to turn out differently than I ever imagined, but I don't think I would trade my life with a person who doesn't have this disease for anything. I realize that many people won't understand why I would say such a thing. Many people automatically assume that I would rather not have MS. The truth is, MS is probably the easiest disease with which to live. It is not contagious, it is not fatal, and does not distort my body in any gruesome way. MS is lifetime disease, but the social isolation that I sometimes feel can be countered by getting out of the house more often. Yes, I have aches and pains each day and night, but who doesn't? This is the life God gave me, now it's up to me to do something with it.

VARIOUS SHADES OF GRAY

W hich things do I want my children to remember from their childhoods? There are many moments that I hope they will recall fondly as the years pass them by, and age turns their hair to lovely shades of grey. I regret that I'll never know our children as adults with grey, almost white hair. At least I'm imagining it will be white, and not a dirty yellow color that some women of age sport. Or the purplish-grey hue that many women of a certain age retain through dyes and tints, making them feel as though they look younger than their actual age. My mother has white hair, as did her mother before her. My hair is gradually becoming more salt than pepper in color, and I'm hoping that it will become the beautiful snow-white color that my mom proudly wears as a crown on atop her head.

I really hope that my daughters will remember the good times we had as a family, both at home, as well as while we were vacationing. One incident that I remember fondly involves a huge box of jelly beans and Steve's new truck. We had gone to New Mexico for Christmas to visit

Steve's family, and a family member had given us a huge box of assorted jelly beans for our 24-hour drive back to Arkansas. I distinctly recall announcing to the kids,

"Let's wait until we get home to open these," I cautioned as the girls reached for the shrink-wrapped box of 1000 assorted jelly beans. "I don't want them to spill all over your dad's new truck, where they might get squished onto the floor." I should have known that my cautionary advice would be unheeded. On our way back home, as we were leaving Albuquerque, Steve pulled into the parking lot of a CVS Pharmacy to get some cold/allergy relief medication for himself for the long drive home.

"Oh, my gosh! I am going to have to get something to help with this sinus pain so I can continue to drive tonight!" Steve exclaimed as he slammed the door to the truck and walked toward the entrance.

"Mom why doesn't Dad just let me drive some of the way?" asked Hunter, who was our oldest and still relatively a new driver.

"Hunter, your dad just bought the truck and the insurance company does not have you listed as a driver yet, and if we had an accident it could be very costly. It's not as if we don't trust your driving skills," I tiredly mentioned to her. "Besides, it's supposed to start snowing heavily at any time now, and he has a lot more experience driving in snow than any of us does."

"I bet that I would be a better driver than Dad is now that he is be sick and on meds," she reluctantly acquiesced, as was always a reminder of her level of intelligence and awareness.

Steve had spent most of the previous day on the ski

slope, attempting to show both girls that snow skiing is an enjoyable pastime. As a result, he had succumbed to whatever virus was making its way around town at the time. Staying in the truck with the girls while Steve went inside the store, I heard what sounded like marbles being poured out in the truck.

Sloan had decided that she would simply reach into the box of jelly beans to discreetly slip one or two out of the package to eat while Steve was in the store. Although she managed to take the shrink-wrapped plastic off the box without calling attention to herself, her discretion ended when she took the top off the jelly bean box and 1000 assorted jelly beans that had once been separated into individual compartments, with labels listing the flavors, showered onto the floorboard of the truck, sounding as though the weather had begun hailing inside the cab.

The girls jumped out of the truck, and began sweeping the candies out onto the parking lot with their hands, so that Steve wouldn't get mad when he returned from his shopping expedition. He was already sick, and none of us wanted to intentionally irritate him.

Upon their return to the warmth of the truck's cab, I reminded them that their dad would most likely see the candies when he returned to the truck, and would wonder how 1000 jelly beans had found their way to the parking lot. Upon hearing this, the girls jumped out of the tuck once again to scatter the jelly beans away from the truck by kicking them under other cars in the lot and into a nearby snow bank. All this time, I sat in the warm truck laughing hysterically, as usual. Once Steve returned, my laughter subsided quickly, and we continued our trip.

That is, until Steve braked for traffic and a lone jelly bean rolled from the back of his Super Cab Ram truck to come to a rest beside Steve's right foot. The laughter returned in earnest at this time until tears were rolling down all of our cheeks. Steve didn't understand why we were laughing, so we told him about the jelly beans, and we all had a good laugh. It's these types of memories that I want my daughters to have imbedded in their memories, because I know that I do, and the thought of 1000 jelly beans scattered in a parking lot in New Mexico still brings a big smile to my lips.

Another time we had a moment with candy was once when we were taking the ferry to Dauphin Island in Mississippi. We took this ferry often when we travelled to the Gulf Coast, so this time I had prepared to allow the kids the fun of feeding the seagulls with bread on the ride over. Once again, I remained in the car as Steve and the girls walked around the ferry, feeding the seagulls. Sloan, in her attempt to fling the bread high, hit her hand on the railing and immediately started screaming in pain. She ran over to where I was sitting in the car, and attempted to receive my sympathy by opening my door so that I could give her a much-needed hug. I had forgotten that I had placed a huge bag of hard candy that I had brought along on the trip to tide us over between meals between my lower leg and the car door. Once she opened the door, the entire bag of candy spilled out onto the surface of the ferry. Upon seeing this happen, Steve yelled across the ferry,

"Get the candy, Nan, pick it up!" as he worried that someone might step on it, and fall.

Sloan was wailing about losing the "precious" candy as well as still crying over her injury, Hunter was appalled that her parents were calling loudly to one another about candy, and Steve was concerned that someone might slip on the candy and then sue us for their injuries. Me? I was doing what I usually do in these types of situations; I laughed without self control! We had managed to turn a simple ferry ride into a circus act! This is referred by us as The Candy Fiasco.

Yes, there are several of these stories; most of them don't involve candy or food of any type. I only hope that our children can remember the fun times that we have had as a family. In fact, once they had me convinced that I was hearing voices when the three of us were gathered around the bar for an evening meal. Steve was working, so I had prepared a meal for the girls and myself. As we were talking and eating, Hunter began mumbling under her breath. Occasionally, I would catch a word or two of what she was saying. She continued to hold conversations with Sloan and me, but her lips were not moving as she said these under-the-breath things, until suddenly I shrieked,

"Oh, no, girls I'm hearing voices and I think I'm going crazy, do you hear them, too?"

Both kids feigned innocence, and told me no, they didn't hear anything, until I picked up the telephone to call Steve at work to let him know that he needed to come home. At this time, our eldest began laughing, and I realized that she had been talking the entire time, and I wasn't going crazy. Sloan had joined her older sister in the merriment—at my sake. We refer to this incident as the time Mom Almost Heard Dead People.

It is these types of memories that I hope they will treasure in their hearts. The ones above, as well as the memory of the time we went to Galveston, TX for spring break. We had gotten a rather late start for the drive to the Gulf that morning, and as a result, our hotel had given away our reservations to another family. It was almost midnight when we finally found a motel with a vacancy. I'll admit it wasn't a brand name motel, but it looked clean and had reasonable rates, so we decided to stay there for the night. Hunter was the first to comment on the aroma in the room,

"This perfume smells good, mom," she said as Steve and I stopped in our tracks to sniff the air. Upon further investigation, Steve located the source of the aroma two doors down from our room. It seems two rooms full of college kids were getting an early start to their Spring Break vacations. We soon began loading our luggage back into the minivan.

"Sweetheart, that's not perfume" Steve told both kids as we pulled away, "You smelled marijuana, and that is illegal. It's a drug and we don't want you around that at your age." Thus began the first of many talks about the dangers of drugs, but definitely not the last. We call this memory, the Motel with the Perfume.

We were forced to drive another hour and half until we found a brand-new motel, one with a known brand name. We were all so tired by this time that I don't even remember unpacking the minivan, we just opened a room door and crashed. In the morning, Steve took the kids down to the lobby for breakfast and let me sleep. I really needed this, I thought, and Steve is a good husband to take the girls to breakfast.

Suddenly, at that moment, sparks fell onto the bed from the light fixture above, while at the same time the television lost power. I panicked, and attempted to reach the telephone beside the bed. This was our first vacation with me in a wheelchair, and the wheelchair was across the room from me. I was so weak from our late night the night before that I couldn't even reach the phone. So here I was, on vacation with my family, trying to rest in a nice motel room, and my bed is going to catch fire from all the sparks! To top it off, I am disabled and cannot reach my wheelchair or a telephone. I lay back in bed, and prayed Steve and the girls would be back from breakfast soon.

Upon their return to the room 30 minutes later, they stood in the doorway and listened to my harrowing tale of the events that had transpired while they were happily eating the complimentary muffins provided by the hotel. Needless to say, we only stay at Hilton's, Hampton Inn's or Embassy Suites now! When I had finished my tirade, Sloan looked up at me and quite innocently said,

"I brought you a muffin, mom," as she took a half-eaten muffin from behind her back. "I kinda got hungry on the way to your room." This episode is referred to as The Time Mom Experienced Sparks in Bed, but not the good kind!

Of course, not every memory is from a vacation where something has gone wrong, there are several memories of everyday life that help complete our memory books. For example, the New Year's Eve that we had taken the girls to a movie and to eat, and upon returning home, I fell out of my wheelchair. We discovered later that my leg was broken; in fact, I had 4 breaks in my right leg and ankle. I was so tired, I told them to let me sleep, and they could take me to the hospital in the morning. My vote on that was rapidly overridden, and I spent the next 3 months in a rehab hospital, an hour away from home. So, I finally received my relaxing moments in bed, but I was awakened each morning at 7:00 to begin physical therapy. I refer to those months in the hospital as my Working Vacation.

Another memorable moment came one summer when Steve had a pile of 2x4's outside our house, because he had decided to become Mr. DIY and take on several projects for our home. Hunter was chasing after our cat, which happened to be an indoor cat that loved to sneak outdoors at every opportunity that came her way. We had asked Hunter to get the cat inside before we left home for the evening. As Hunter crouched down to call the cat, the feline made a lunge for freedom. Hunter quickly leapt for the cat, not realizing her dad had stacked the 2x4's right where the cat was heading. The entire debacle resulted in Hunter receiving a huge bruise on her forehead, and the cat a few more hours outside. Until the bruise healed, Steve called her "Anakin Skywalker" for the Star Wars character with an almost identical facial scar. We still refer to that incident as the time Hunter tried out for Star Wars!

Those same 2x4's became a monstrosity that we lovingly called The Green Box once it was completed to sit in our front yard. It was supposed to be a receptacle for holding our trash once it had been tied and discarded. That way, the garbage men wouldn't have to bend over as far to pace the bags of trash into the truck on garbage day, and it would hopefully deter wild animals from getting into our garbage. It sounded like a good idea to me when Steve told me his plan. That was before I saw the completed project. Steve, in his earnestness to build something useful, had built the box large enough to hold a small car! He moved it into place using my dad's tractor and it sat outside our house in the country for several years. I mockingly named it The Green Box as a tribute to the Boston Red Sox and their outfield, which is lovingly called by many baseball fans, The Green Monster!

Yet another memory is the time we were at the Little Rock Zoo and Steve inadvertently managed to dump me out of the zoo's wheelchair that I was using for the day. He had thought it would be fun to race the girls to the Gibbon exhibit, while pushing me in the loaner wheelchair provided by the zoo. This was an impromptu race, and I had no say in the matter. The girls trotted ahead of us, laughing and giggling toward a bridge that marked the entrance to the Primate Exhibit.

Suddenly I felt my body go airborne as the wheelchair's tires went over a drainage pipe in the pavement and then I landed with a thud right behind some elderly zoo patrons, who turned their heads to look at us in shock and horror. I was bent over laughing silently, so all they could see were my shoulders shaking. They panicked, and called for help from a zoo employee, who rushed to my side to see how he could help.

By this time, I was getting up on my own, and still laughing at the situation, much to the onlookers' shock. My laughter was infectious, and the girls and Steve and I were all standing there laughing hysterically at the situation.

What else could I do? It was funny! After reassuring the employee and other patrons that I was in fact all right, and my husband was truly sorry, we resumed our visit to the zoo. The memory is called The Time Dad Dumped Mom from the Wheelchair.

All of these memories include the entire family, with only one that includes the inanimate member of the family which is my wheelchair. I try to make it a point that my wheelchair is not the focus of family outings, but treat it instead as though it is an appendage, without which I cannot function. It is a fact of life, in much the same way the way that we get wet when it rains is a fact of our lives.

My daughters have grown up seeing me in a wheelchair, and I like to think that it has made them into more caring people. People that will pause to hold a door open for someone who needs it, or people that will help someone in the need of assistance in other ways. It is those moments that I want them to remember most of all; the moments when they see someone in need of a hand, so that they will take the time out of their busy days to help someone less fortunate than they may be.

That is all I need for my mind to rest easily. It doesn't matter what color their hair becomes with age, or even mine for that matter. I only ask that our children mature into caring, compassionate adults with a reverence and love for God. I already know that they will be amazing adults; in fact, they already are on their way.

I realize that not every memory is a funny one, but those are the ones that I hope our daughters will remember the most. We have had numerous pets to join our family, and most of them were around until old age took them from us. We have a small plot of land where the pets are buried, with stones found at the creek to mark each grave, and where the ground is shaded by Oak trees in the spring and summer, and blanketed with multi-colored leaves and acorns each fall and winter.

There are memories galore from each holiday spent together, be it canoe races at the pond on July Fourth, to awesome fireworks displays each July, to hayrides with friends and cousins, followed by ooey, gooey, delicious S'mores toasted over outdoor fires, and the Christmases spent with the family building a 9-foot snowman, or sledding down the hills of Fire Tower Road, and even those moments spent snow skiing, or scuba diving. I've finally come to the realization that I cannot dictate which memories will fill the minds of my children, but I can make sure they have plenty of happy ones from which to choose.

HEREDITY AND MS: THE GENETIC RIPPLE

I've always said that I don't need a cure, but my one wish would be to eradicate MS from the world in my children's lifetimes. Whenever I hear of someone I know is diagnosed with this disease, I pray for them first of all, because I know that even with new medicines to treat the symptoms, that person will need the Lord even more than before. My greatest fear has always been for my daughters to be diagnosed with MS. My daughters have a greater than normal chance of being diagnosed with MS than the general public does, but it's not that much. I know my daughters fear being diagnosed with a disease such as MS, because they have seen the struggles I have had to face in my daily life. Not all the struggles have been monumental, but one in particular sticks out in my mind.

It happened one summer when our daughters were about 8 and 4 and we had taken them to a small theme park about an hour from our home to spend the day. It just so happened that this theme park doesn't charge admission for persons in wheelchairs. Steve and the girls went in the gates, showing their season passes, while I stood back for a park employee to open the gate for me. It just so happened that a large group was behind me. Judging from their shirts, it was a family reunion. The eldest gentleman in the group boldly remarked,

"Boy, I wish I was in a wheelchair so I could get in for free!"

The words alone didn't disturb me, but the fact that he was surrounded by his adult children and young grandchildren did. I was shocked that he would say something so blatantly prejudiced against all handicapped visitors to the park. He voiced his statement rather loudly, so that his entire family of about 20 people could hear. If I had my wits about me, I would have said something along the lines of,

"I will gladly trade my wheelchair for your legs any time." But I didn't think of saying that until much later, when the man was not around. A few of his adult children acted embarrassed by his words, and offered me a shrug of their shoulders and a sympathetic smile. I would have felt much better about the entire incident had one of his adult children taken the time to point out to the ten or twelve children that were with the group the fact that their grandfather was wrong for saying what he did. That was a teachable moment that was lost. I vowed to myself not to let moments such as this to slip by without making a comment. Not necessarily a rude comment, but something to say so that other people will know not to say those types of things.

I think because of that incident, I am more aware of what I might say in public. My mother in law shared with me just the other day that something I'd said to her one day nearly 19 years before still rings in her ears today. I remember the day well: our youngest daughter was an infant and I had scheduled an appointment with her pediatrician. Jan had offered to help me get the girls to the doctor's office the day before, so I had the girls dressed and ready to go before Jan got to our house.

At the time, Jan was an instructor at a local teaching medical university, and she was running late that day, which made me a little uptight. I detest being late for appointments. It was raining, and cold, so traffic was not the best that day. I was driving the van recklessly, trying to make it to the appointment on time.

I remember Jan looking at me and asking me to pull over. I pulled the van into a parking lot, turned to Jan, and she quietly explained that doctor's offices almost expect their patients to be late on rainy days such as this. Her calm and reassuring voice broke through the tension in the van, and I began crying. I placed my hands over my face, and told her that I was just now realizing that I was dependent upon other people to help me take my children to the doctor, and it was upsetting to me.

After a few moments of comforting words and a much-needed hug from my mother in law, we continued to the appointment at a reasonable speed. It just so happened that Jan had been right all along, and once we made it to the doctor's office we still had to wait about 15 minutes before seeing the doctor. Jan says that ever since that day she has looked at the fact that I have MS and am dependent on others for things that most people take for granted in a completely different light.

That's exactly what I mean about watching what you say to people. The incident could have turned real ugly that day, with me blaming Jan for being late, and blaming the weather for not cooperating, and blaming my MS on everything else that had gone wrong in my life. All I really needed at the time was an understanding ear and a hug! I thank God daily for bringing not only Steve into my life, but his mom, too! I can't ask for a better mother in law.

As well as loosening up on my definitions of how Hunter should dress, I think that Carla, Katarina, and Beth helped in other ways, too. Often, we would pick our kids up after their day at Child's Day Out and take them to a local farmer's market, museum, or the zoo.

I think that helped in other ways, too. For example, I was most likely to be the only mother in my children's preschool and elementary classrooms with a walker, cane, or a wheelchair. That fact never seemed to bother my children much at all; they just accepted the fact that I was disabled. They didn't know me in any other way. I was the room mother for Hunter's kindergarten and first grade classes and went to her school weekly to read, craft, or just be another warm body in the room. I treasured those days, mainly because I realized just how much of a difference a little attention some of these kids were hungering, and what an enormous difference a weekly visit to a classroom can make.

I like to think that I touched other kids' lives, as well as my own. Each year, toward the beginning of the school year my visit would include information on Multiple Sclerosis. I definitely didn't want my girls to feel left out or different in any way simply because they had a mom that couldn't walk. I also like to think that my presence in the classrooms might have helped to lessen the amount of prejudice that all of the kids would grow up with. I wanted them to each see that I was normal, and could give hugs just as well from a sitting position as others can by standing!

Sometimes the students would be timid to be near me, but I always informed them that MS was not "catching". After they understood that, I would give and receive more hugs than I could count! The hours I spent in my daughters' classrooms were some of the most fulfilling, and almost made me wish that I had become a teacher myself-- I said almost!

The Arkansas chapter of the National Multiple Sclerosis Society helped by giving me pamphlets and coloring books to take to the classes on several occasions. I felt like a one-person public relations team, trying to get information to the public on the disease that I know far too well.

It's not easy to explain Multiple Sclerosis. There can be 1,000 people with the disease; each person will be experiencing different symptoms. Not just slightly different, but some differences can be quite vast. For example, I cannot handle the heat and humidity of Arkansas summers, while some people with MS find the heat comforting to their symptoms. If I am in Arkansas during the summer, I spend the days and nights inside an air-conditioned environment. Is it any wonder that autumn is my favorite time of the year? Spring is nice too, but the threat of 100°+ days, coupled with high humidity, is always on the horizon. Autumn brings with it the promise of cooler weather as well as my favorite time of year, the holiday season. I have always loved the Christmas season, because of the sense of family and wonderment that pervades each and every moment of this time of year.

Finding Your Cause

The pain was excruciating. I had never before felt pain this intense. Okay, I had given birth to two children years earlier, but at least labor pain had a purpose to it. This lower back pain that was coursing through my body offered no such reward. What had started out as what I assumed were sympathy pains for my niece, who had gone into labor with her second child earlier in the day, had now progressed past a backache to a BACKACHE. I couldn't find a comfortable position no matter how I shifted in my wheelchair.

"Sloan, I need to go to bed," I whined to my 16-year-old-daughter. She dutifully wheeled me into my bedroom, got the standing lift for me, and placed me into what I was hoping to be a safe, soft, place to relax the backache pain away. It was neither safe nor soft, because before she even left the room, I was in tears.

"I can't take this," I said through my tears, coming through as a full-fledged whine at this point.

"Mom, I don't know how to help you!" Sloan exclaimed, her frustration becoming evident to me.

Her frustration only caused me to cry harder. Sloan retrieved the lift from the closet once again, placed the vest around my torso, and lifted me back into my chair. After she had situated me in my chair, I was sobbing, giving Sloan another reason to worry. *What if my pain kept increasing? Where was Steve, when I needed him?* The stress that my pain was causing her was evident on her face. With her brow furrowed, she stood before me and made a decision that would in due course save my life.

"Mom, I know you don't want to go, but we are going to the hospital," Sloan's voice was strong with conviction, "Now, not later." At that moment, I arched my back from the pain that was overtaking my body and slipped from my wheelchair to the floor with a solid thud.

"Call Bibbi and Pop," I practically barked the instruction to her. I was hoping they were not too tired from the day's gathering of extended family at our pond that day. The family had gathered for a typical weekend cookout at the pond, which we do often in the summer months. It is always a fun time seeing all of my nieces and nephews enjoy the outdoors playing horseshoes, tetherball, fishing, swimming, and catching Frisbee's.

By now, it was getting close to 9:00 p.m., and Steve had yet to return from a quick scuba trip to the large lake on the other side of town. He knows that I worry about him whenever he dives alone, but he loves diving so much, that sometimes he doesn't have a choice. In instances such as these, we always kept in touch via phone so that I would at least know when and where he was diving. On this day, I knew he has gone to De Gray Lake, in a large state park located only 5 miles west of Arkadelphia. Sloan quickly called my parents who rushed to our house to help me into my wheelchair once again.

As soon as I was situated in my chair, my dad helped Sloan get me to the van. Sloan buckled my chair securely in place, then we were on our way to the hospital. Steve called then to say he was on the way home. Sloan told him to meet us at the emergency room, because I was sick. I was throwing up by this time, and the heaving that was taking over my body left me completely powerless to comprehend anything that was going on, except for this unbelievable pain.

At 16, Sloan had not been driving for very long, but I placed my life in her hands that night as she cautiously drove our van through the dark around curves, hills, bridges, and to the highway that led into town. His concern for me was written all over his face. He wasn't aware of just how sick I was, or even if I was sick, but his doubts vanished the moment he opened the van door as soon as we stopped.

I was assessed in triage, and it was quickly determined that I was experiencing a severe UTI (urinary tract infection), a relatively high fever (105), extremely low blood pressure, and eventually, sepsis (a potentially fatal infection). Luckily, my primary care physician was on call that night and just so happened to be there. As much as I wanted Steve to go home and get some rest before he had to work the next day, I welcomed the comfort of having him nearby me in the ER. He stayed with me the entire night, Sloan did, too.

Neither of them wanted to leave my side, but reluctantly left my bedside vigil at my insistence that they go home to get some much-needed sleep in the early morning hours. My doctor kept me in the ER all night, and it wasn't until the next morning that the tests confirmed that I did, indeed have sepsis. At this point, Dr. Graham came to my bedside and told me that it was imperative that I go to a hospital in Little Rock.

I was slipping in and out of consciousness without even realizing it. As much as I wanted Steve to go home and get some rest before he had to work the next day, I welcomed the comfort of having him nearby me in the ER. He stayed with me the entire night, as did Sloan. Neither of them wanted to leave my side. My doctor kept me in the ER all night, and it wasn't until the next morning the tests confirmed that I did, indeed have sepsis. At this point, Dr. Graham came to my bedside and told me it was imperative I go to a hospital in Little Rock.

I assumed I would be transported by ambulance, and even tried to make some semblance of a joke out of it by saying, "I don't mind going to Little Rock, as long as they don't use the siren!" Dr. Graham simply smiled a half smile, willing me to realize how sick I was. I didn't understand what he was trying to tell me. I thought I would go to the large hospital for a few days, then come back home.

Dr. Graham gave a slight smile, then turned to a nurse and said quite tersely,

"Call Med Flight, if they can't get her to the hospital within an hour, it will be too late."

With those words, I realized just how sick I was. The nurse rushed back into the emergency room where I was waiting for further instructions, and hopefully relief.

"Great news, Dr. Graham," she exclaimed as she hung up the phone. "They are returning to Little Rock right now, they said they could be here in fifteen minutes, tops." And then without wasting a moment, nurses began preparing me to be transported via helicopter to Little Rock.

Within minutes, I had been prepared for the ride, and two EMT's walked into the door just as the nurse finished securing my IV tubing to the side of my bedding. I was aware of all of the commotion surrounding me, but it was as though I was watching it happen to a patient on the set of the television show, *Grey's Anatomy*. The doctors and nurses weren't as handsome or glamourous as the actors that portrayed them on television, but they were just as efficient as they packed me onto the helicopter.

Dr. Graham stood by my side in the parking lot as the helicopter, with me securely in place, took off for the short flight to Little Rock. While we were rising above the hospital, I remember thinking of Steve, and hoping that someone from the hospital would call him to let him know of my relocation. As the helicopter took off from Arkadelphia, I finally realized just how sick I had become.

The flight was a quick one, and I remember the helicopter landing on the large white circle painted with a red H in the middle of it on the roof of the hospital. I even remember being taken out of the helicopter and lying on a gurney covered with blankets and wires under the harsh summer sun, with its excessive heat, and recall thinking to myself, *"Don't they realize how badly heat affects my MS?* Pleading with them through my eyes, to *"get me into the cool confines of the hospital ASAP!!"*

Once there, I was assessed by new doctors and nurses,

and can recall being told I should be in the ICU. The last thing I remember is my bed being pushed down the hall toward a room. That's it. I was unconscious for ten days.

It was during those ten days of unconscious slumber that I received a visit from my mom's sister, Nancy. She had passed away a few months prior to my extended stay in the hospital, but I recall seeing her as clearly as though she were standing in my room. Her wrinkles were gone, as was her gray hair. The wheelchair to which she had been confined towards the end of her life was nowhere in sight. As she moved so gracefully around my bed and all the machines that were keeping me alive, I had never seen my aunt look so beautiful as she sat at the end of my bed, placing her hand very comfortingly on my leg. She looked me in the eyes and said,

"Nancy, you have to stay here. Your family needs you." Those are the only words I remember her speaking to me. She spoke the words to me in a very matter of fact tone, so I didn't question her. I accepted her words as fact.

Even though I can't recall her speaking to me again, it was as though her presence was a calmness that washed over me. I knew I was going to get better. I don't know how, but I knew this wasn't my time to leave this Earth.

I recall an instant feeling of sadness washed over me as I realized I wouldn't be returning to the heavenly life from which she came. I can't explain the feeling exactly, but I knew she was going back to her Heavenly home, and I couldn't go with her. I never saw my aunt's final destination, but I sensed the warmth, light, and beauty emanating from somewhere behind my Aunt Nancy. I wanted to return to that wondrous place with her, and was truly disappointed when she said I couldn't go with her.

In the meantime, I was being kept alive with IV fluids, a breathing tube, and a respirator, as well as 5-7 different antibiotics and other medications. I needed medicine to keep my heart beating at a normal rate, as well as medicine to regulate my blood pressure and a vast assortment of other medications to try to get every system in my body on the same page. By this time, I was under the care of several doctors, and one of them came to Steve that first night,

"Mr. Wayland, I don't know if your wife is strong enough to pull through. She has several infections that we are trying to address, but it's anybody's guess if her body has the strength to overcome everything. Our main concern is that her blood pressure has dropped to 65/30 and this is a result of the Septicemia, which basically means the growth of the infectious material is faster than her body can possibly fight off the infection. Do you know her wishes if she never regains consciousness, have either of you prepared a Living Will, or discussed your wishes should the worst happens?" Steve circled the entire Critical Care Unit of the hospital and pondered what he should do on my behalf. He wandered in shock as he replayed in his mind the grim reality the doctors were telling him.

"I don't really..." Steve managed to say. "We haven't discussed it with one another, but I do know that she doesn't give up easily. She's a fighter, as well as pretty stubborn," he commented, while Sloan stood quietly in the corner of the CCU area, looking much younger than her16 years.

"We'll do what we can to help your wife, but it is

basically up to her if she pulls through or not," Dr. Franklin said. "We are giving her several high doses of antibiotics, as well as medicine to keep her heart rate and blood pressure up. That's about all we can do for her right now."

"Is there any way of knowing how long she will be this way?" Steve inquired.

"Mr. Wayland, I'm just trying to keep the Septicemia in check. It will begin shutting down her organs if we can't stop it from spreading further. I'll be by to check on her in the morning," Dr. Franklin said as he walked out the door. Steve buried his head in his hands as the doctor walked down the hall, stopping briefly to talk with the charge nurse about my care. When he raised his head from his hands, Steve exhaled deeply while wiping tears from his eyes.

It had been several days since he had last rested. Sloan walked to where he was sitting and threw her arms around him. They sat that way for a long moment, until a nurse came to check my vital signs yet again. They watched the nurse as she went through the routine of measuring my vital signs, hoping with all of their hearts that today would be the day I would awaken and flash them a big smile while asking, where's dinner?

Steve placed his arm around Sloan when he saw tears hovering at the tips of her eyelashes ready to spill, onto her cheeks. "Mom's going to beat this, Sloan, she will. Right now, I need to make some phone calls; a lot of people are concerned about her."

The first phone call was to our eldest daughter, Hunter, who was in Madison, Wisconsin for the summer working as an intern in the University of Wisconsin Chemistry department. She wasn't prepared for the news, and Steve tried to gently tell her of my condition.

"But dad," she exclaimed when Steve finished relaying the days' events. "I just talked to her two days ago and she was fine! She said she had a backache, but that was all."

"Oh, Hunter, a lot has happened since then. They even sent her by MedFlight to Little Rock from Arkadelphia." Steve then attempted to fill Hunter in on the previous days' happenings. "She was fine Saturday, but Sloan had to take her to the hospital that night." Hunter responded by saying,

"I'll fly home now," she insisted. "Don't worry about the internship, I'll take care of everything. I need to call and find a flight as soon as possible."

"Hunter, I'm worried you may lose your internship if you come home. Just stay in Wisconsin, and I will keep you informed on mom's progress," Steve cautioned with the slightest hint of hesitation. "Honestly Hunter, mom would want you to stay there. Besides you know how important mom and I feel school is." he continued speaking to her, although he was speaking only to himself.

He was speaking the words he thought he should be saying, but at the same time he wanted nothing more than to be able to hug both daughters tightly.

"Dad, do you think I can accomplish anything while mom is fighting for her life? I'm coming home, and I don't care about the internship. I will let you know when my flight gets in."

The next day, Hunter flew into Little Rock and went directly to the hospital to see me in a hospital bed surrounded by machines beeping and constantly flashing with their multiple colors of lights. Of course, I was oblivious to the attention my condition was receiving. Steve, Hunter, and Sloan stayed with me in the hospital, sleeping in chairs or couches while my mom, dad, and sisters visited daily. The doctors kept monitoring my condition and adjusting my medications as needed.

After a week with little progress in my condition, Steve was once again faced with some difficult decisions as to my care. How much intervention would I want the medical staff to take? At this point, Dr. Franklin came to Steve and stated,

"We have won a large part of the battle, she has responded well to the antibiotics and other medications. Do you have any questions at this point?"

"Well," Steve replied, "I need to understand what has happened so far. Is there any sign of her current brain activity? What are the potential issues with it going on so long, how long will it take for her to regain consciousness, and what are the long-term potential effects of this," Steve asked his questions in rapid-fire succession. He could ask all the right questions thanks to his mom, who teaches nursing students at the University of New Mexico in Albuquerque.

Unfortunately, the answers to those questions were not so forthcoming.

"Her brain activity is not clear at this point, because of all the medications and the effects of the dying bacterial infection are both still a real threat at this point. We will know more in the next 36 hours as her body begins to rid itself of the toxins being produced from the dying infectious materials."

"Is this why her body is so swollen and bloated now? I hardly recognize her with all the swelling, it is unreal," Steve mentioned. He was thinking to himself if only the doctors knew what kind of woman I was inside this swollen, sickened body and that maybe, just maybe they would be able to help more.

"The swelling is a good sign, because it means that the infectious disease is losing the battle and Nancy's immune system is winning. You will notice a lot of drainage through her kidneys over the next few days," Dr. Franklin answered. Over the next 4-5 days, my body released much of the accumulated fluids in my system, and I lost close to 50 pounds.

Sloan later told me that whenever my dad would visit and stand beside my bed, he would speak to me in his low tones. She said I would react to his voice and touch, by attempting to open my eyes and turning my head toward his voice.

"Those movements gave me hope that you would be okay," she said not long ago, while recalling the events of June 2014. "I think it helped Pop, too. He would hold your hand and talk to you as if you could hear him."

After ten days of being unconscious, the nurses began removing my breathing tube since I had begun breathing on my own, and the nurse asked me to lean forward and cough. I did, and the breathing tube came out in one fell swoop. According to Steve, I then said,

"I am really hungry for a hamburger," for no reason whatsoever.

The nurses and Steve laughed, while I said, "Did I say that? I'm not even hungry! I then rested my head on the pillow and promptly fell asleep. When I awakened hours later, I turned to who I assumed was a nurse in my room and asked her,

"Could you please find my husband?"

The "nurse" quickly left my room to find Steve. When Steve got to my room, he told me the nurse was actually my eldest child. I had mistaken Hunter for a nurse! She came back to my room then and I assured her yes, knew who she was, and I recognize her, it's just everything momentarily had become confused.

I knew I recognized her in some way, I simply couldn't comprehend she was my daughter and was here instead of in Wisconsin, where she should be. I know this episode alone struck fear in my family's hearts. *Had I lost the ability to recall family members? What other deficits would I exhibit?* Within a day or two, my mind was straight once again. For the next week, doctors and nurses kept coming by my room, peering in, and then proclaiming,

"Mrs. Wayland! It's so good to see you awake," or other such exclamation, before introducing themselves as someone with whom I had come into contact when I was first admitted to the hospital. It never ceased to amaze me at the number of people who would stop by my room. One day after such an occurrence happened, the head nurse on my floor commented I really hadn't been expected to survive.

It wasn't until then I realized just how sick I had been. Slowly, I was recovering from my ordeal, grateful to God for seeing me through this episode. I also gave the doctors and nurses a very heart-felt thank you, for all their hard work, many times over. I have always held people in the health profession in high esteem. I do so even more now! I can't imagine how my family had felt the entire time I was unconscious.

I am grateful to God for allowing me to remain on Earth. I know I said that I experienced feelings of sadness and despair when I realized I had to come back from the most glorious heaven I ever imagined. I no longer have those feelings and I am glad I never reached the afterlife.

I find comfort in knowing what awaits me and others who accept Christ into their lives, and it gives me strength for every day. I treasure the experience and I am glad to know when my time comes to exit this world, I will assume my place in Heaven. I am surer of this than ever before.

I was in the hospital for over two months, during which time I underwent multiple surgeries for a diseased gall bladder, breast cancer, and kidney stones. I am happy to say my MS did not return, not even for a hint of a relapse, during this time. My neurologist has no explanation for that because typically any type of infection causes my MS to exacerbate.

I believe God knows just how much our bodies can take, and the summer of 2014 showed me that my body can handle a lot! I believe I wouldn't have survived all the infections, surgeries, and so forth without God being first and foremost in my life. God is so good!

I recall almost nothing of the flight. I remember landing on the large red H on the roof of the hospital in Little Rock, being wheeled through the emergency room and down a long hallway to a room in the ICU. The cool air inside the hospital was a welcome relief from the searing sunshine and overpowering humidity that enveloped the atmosphere outside.

By the time the helicopter landed in Little Rock, my blood pressure had dropped even further, and I was being evaluated by an entirely new set of doctors and nurses. After starting new IV lines for the antibiotics and other fluids, I overheard the nurses speaking to one another about a patient with "the worst case of sepsis" they had ever seen, only to come to the realize that *I* was the patient with sepsis. The last thing I remember, the nurse was adjusting the blinds on my west-facing window, so as the sun would not shine directly in my eyes.

I remained in a comatose state for ten days, during which time I later discovered that Steve had been faced with several decisions regarding my care. He later told me that he was so frightened he would lose me during this time. My parents and sisters, as well as other friends and family members came to visit me while I remained unconscious. There were many people in Arkadelphia and Arkansas in general keeping me in their thoughts and prayers. I later discovered that through the power of Facebook my name had been added to prayer lists around the county.

It was at one point during these ten days, I had a visit from my Aunt Nancy, who had passed away months earlier. She sat at the foot of my bed, rubbing my leg and talking to me. I remember her telling me that even though she knew I wanted to go with her, it was not possible.

"It's not your time," Aunt Nancy said to me, "You need to stay here for your girls."

I remember a profound sense of sadness that overtook me, a sense of loss that was foreign to me. It was beautiful behind Aunt Nancy, and I could hear choirs of angels singing. I can recall having a sense of warmth, as though it was my home, but I wasn't allowed to stay.

In the meantime, Steve and Sloan had made their way to Little Rock, where they were surprised to find me unconscious in the ICU. Steve had been speaking with his mother by telephone, and she gave him the questions to ask the doctors when he saw them. She offered to fly out, but she had obligations in New Mexico that prevented her from coming to Arkansas. She did the next best thing by giving Steve the questions to ask concerning my care. Steve's primary concern was the extent of lasting effects that may be apparent after awakening after being unconscious for so long.

Unfortunately, the answers to those questions were not so forthcoming.

"Her brain activity is not clear at this point, because of all the medications and the effects of the dying bacterial infection are both still a real threat at this point. We will know more in the next 36 hours as her body begins to rid itself of the toxins being produced form the dying infectious materials."

"Is this why her body is so swollen and bloated now? I hardly recognize her with all the swelling, it is unreal," Steve mentioned. He was thinking to himself if only the doctors knew what kind of woman I was inside this swollen, sickened body that maybe, just maybe they would be able to help more.

"The swelling is a good sign, because it means that the infectious disease is losing the battle and Nancy's immune system is winning. You will notice a lot of drainage through her kidneys over the next few days," Dr. Franklin answered. Over the next 4-5 days, my body released much of the accumulated fluids in my system, and I lost close to 50 pounds.

Sloan later told me whenever my dad would visit and stand beside my bed, he would speak to me in his low tones. She said I would react to his voice and touch, by attempting to open my eyes and turning my head toward his voice.

"Those movements gave me hope that you would be okay," she said not long ago, while recalling the events of June 2014. "I think it helped Pop, too. He would hold your hand and talk to you as if you could hear him."

After ten days of being unconscious, the nurses began removing my breathing tube since I had begun breathing on my own, and the nurse asked me to lean forward and cough. I did, and the breathing tube came out in one fell swoop. According to Steve, I then said,

"I am really hungry for a hamburger," for no reason whatsoever.

The nurses and Steve laughed, while I said, "Did I say that? I'm not even hungry! I then rested my head on the pillow and promptly fell asleep. When I awakened hours later, I turned to who I assumed was a nurse in my room and asked her, "Could you please find my husband?"

The "nurse" quickly left my room to find Steve. When

Steve got to my room, he told me the nurse was actually our eldest child. I had mistaken Hunter for a nurse! She came back to my room then and I assured her yes, knew who she was, and I recognize her, it's just everything momentarily had become confused.

I knew I recognized her in some way, I simply couldn't comprehend she was my daughter and was here instead of in Wisconsin, where she should be. I know this episode alone struck fear in my family's hearts. *Had I lost the ability to recall family members? What other deficits would I exhibit?* Within a day or two, my mind was straight once again. For the next week, doctors and nurses kept coming by my room, peering in, and then proclaiming,

"Mrs. Wayland! It's so good to see you awake," or other such exclamation, before introducing themselves as someone with whom I had come into contact when I was first admitted to the hospital. It never ceased to amaze me at the number of people who would stop by my room. One day after such an occurrence happened, the head nurse on my floor commented I really hadn't been expected to survive.

It wasn't until then I realized just how sick I had been. Slowly, I was recovering from my ordeal, grateful to God for seeing me through this episode. I also gave the doctors and nurses a very heart-felt thank you, for all their hard work, many times over. I have always held people in the health profession in high esteem. I do so even more now!

I remained in the hospital for another 2 months, but was able to come home for my family's annual July 4th bash at the pond. The rest of the summer was spent in and out of the hospital as doctors removed a diseased gall bladder, a lump from my breast, and attempted 18 times to blast an extremely large kidney stone.

I am grateful to God for allowing me to remain on Earth. I know I said that I experienced feelings of sadness and despair when I realized I had to come back from the most glorious heaven I ever imagined. I no longer have those feelings and I am glad I never reached the afterlife. I find comfort in knowing it what awaits me and others who accept Christ into their lives, and it gives me strength for every day. I treasure the experience and I am glad to know when my time comes to exit this world, I will assume my place in Heaven. I am surer of this than ever before.

I am very happy to say my MS did not return, not even for a hint of a relapse, during this time. My neurologist has no explanation for that, because usually any type of infection causes my MS to exacerbate. I believe God knows just how much our bodies can take, and the summer of 2014 showed me that my body can handle a lot! I believe I wouldn't have survived all the infections, surgeries, and so forth without God being first and foremost in my life. God is so good.

The day following my return from the coma, a different doctor came to my room. She was tall, attractive, and very personable. She held her hand out to me as she walked into my room. Her smart, black heels clicked on the linoleum floor as she spanned the distance from the door to my bedside.

"Hello, Nancy," she stated as she strode into my room with brisk steps. "I'm Dr. Wallace, and I'll be seeing you after your lumpectomy next week."

What?? Excuse me? I looked at her with what I assume

was an expression of confusion. She laughed an abrupt laugh, upon seeing my confusion.

"They haven't told you? The doctors found a suspicious mass in your right breast when they looked at your chest x-ray upon admission," she explained. With that, she explained that after the removal of the suspicious cells, they would be tested to see if they are malignant.

"Depending on those results," she further explained, "we will discuss further treatments, regarding chemotherapy or radiation. And after that, I will work with you to determine our next course of action." I sat in bewilderment as she walked out of the room, my mind spinning. I sat in my bed, going over the last conversation in my mind. Steve and Sloan returned from dinner at that time, and sat in the chairs provided for visitors, as I turned to speak to Steve.

"So, what's this about breast cancer," I questioned Steve as soon as soon as he walked in the door to my room. It came out much more abruptly than I had intended. I simply wanted answers to all the questions running through my mind. Steve patiently explained to me that I would need several surgeries before I could consider this latest health crisis over.

This was completely new territory for me. In my 50 years of life, I had been hospitalized only twice before, not including the births of my two daughters. I had my tonsils removed at age four, which I remembered mainly for the ice cream I could consume as a part of my recovery, and had fallen from my wheelchair upon returning from an evening out celebrating the New Year with Steve and the girls in 2011 that had resulted in my leg being broken multiple times.

Other than those two times, and my diagnosis of MS in '86 and the births of our daughters in '93 and '97. I have been a relatively healthy woman. I think that is one reason the news of the kidney stones, gall bladder disease, and breast cancer came as such a shock to me. That, and although I come from a large family, there had not been one person diagnosed with breast cancer on either side of my family, going back at least five generations.

I accept the challenge of being a first-generation breast cancer patient calmly, but no one who knows me escapes my urging for them to get mammograms. So now I am becoming an advocate for breast cancer awareness, as well as an outspoken advocate for Multiple Sclerosis. Although I carry this new label, I am ardent in my prayers, thanking God for allowing the causes to come to me to be a voice for them.

I gladly speak up against several causes, and will happily lend my voice against domestic violence, child abuse, animal abuse, and I support the trials of public school teachers in our country as well as earthquake relief in Nepal. I could fill this page with all the worthy causes that I support, but it will take more than just one person speaking up for those less fortunate than ourselves, but maybe, just maybe I can be a voice inside the minds of many to lend your voices, time, and yes, whatever financial support you are able to give to any of the worthy causes that could use your support.

At exactly the same month of the following year, I was getting ready for bed. When I removed my bra, I was startled to feel a tender spot on my right breast, about two inches from the surgical scar from the lumpectomy of 12 months ago.

"Steve, " I called out to him, all the while testing the tenderness of the anomaly under my arm with the pads of my forefingers.

"Could you please come in here?"

"I'll be right there, Nan," he answered mindlessly. I heard him open the bedroom door before he said anything else. "What's up? Are you stressing about Sloan's birthday again? I told you we would make it special for her, don't we always?" He was talking to my back, so I turned toward him and stated,

"No, it's not that. Come over here and feel this."

He walked quickly to my bedside to see what was going on.

"There is something wrong, babe, I don't know what it is," I said nervously. At this point my heart began to race, thinking to myself of the worst possible case scenario: Cancer, again. Steve, ever the optimist, sat on the edge of the bed to gingerly palpate the lump. It was a little tender, so I pushed his hand away, saying,

"Oh, it's nothing" as I pulled the sheet over my shoulders. I was tired, and was ready to sleep.

"No, it's not nothing, Nan, but it's probably an insect bite or something. We have been outside all day."

As I pondered his response, I suddenly remembered that I had been wearing a new bra that day.

"Yeah, you're probably right. Besides, I was wearing a new bra and it's probably just an irritant from the fabric or something." We put the idea of Breast Cancer in the back of our minds and watched a classic movie, *When Harry Met Sally.*

The next morning, an insect bite on my breast didn't make sense to me in the same way that it had the night before. As I was showering, I fully inspected the mysterious lump. The more I looked at it, the more it *did* resemble like a bug bite.

"C'mon Nancy," I said as I was drying off. Steve poked his head in the bathroom, looking around to see who I had been talking to. I laughed as he ducked his head out of the bathroom, and told him,

"No, I don't have a mysterious visitor in here with me, unless you count the cat!"

He chuckled and told my cat,

"Curie, Mom has finally gone crazy," as he made his way to the kitchen for coffee. Leaving me with an audience of my cat to watch me dress.

After breakfast, I couldn't shake an uneasy feeling that I had. *It must be all the changes that are happening,* I thought to myself. Hunter was graduating with her Bachelors of Science degree and was torn between several schools that wanted her for her Master's and possibly Doctoral degrees, I had received my Master of Arts in English and Creative Writing, we had been looking into the possibilities of having my book published, and Sloan was also finished with High School and was looking forward to beginning her Freshman year at the school her dad and sister were graduates from.

It wasn't until a week later as I undressed for bed once again that I even remembered the insect bite. I glanced down at my breast to see if it had healed. Imagine my shock when I saw that it had become much larger, and more tender. I had stopped wearing a bra around the house, and the insect bite didn't itch or anything. I sat on the bed to call Steve at work.

I quickly called his number at work, and when he answered, I didn't even tell him my reason for calling, I simply blurted out,

"I think it's cancer."

Steve put me on hold for what seemed an eternity, before he was back with,

"Nan, calm down. What do you think is cancer, and when did you get a medical license?"

"Steve, I'm not kidding. Seriously. What we thought was an insect bite is now a monstrous, angry sore!"

"Nancy, I'm not working late tonight, and I'll be home as soon as I can."

After another eternity, Steve came home, saw my "bug bite" and said,

"We will go get that looked at tomorrow, but for now try your best not to worry too much." Though I wasn't pleased with his reaction, I settled into bed to watch my go-to for relaxing; re-runs of *Friends* episodes. Although I had all ten seasons of the sitcom on DVD, I enjoyed the reruns on television, as it was often a surprise which episode would come next, as they are not shown in the same order as when they were first filmed. I take joy in such small pleasantries such as this.

WE'VE COME A LONG WAY, BABIES

I t was an epiphany. It came upon me quite slowly, yet as explosive as a firework.

I know that I'm not ready for it yet, but I can see it coming in force. In some ways, I have been preparing for it for 24 years. What, you may ask? An empty nest. Yes, as I sat in the hospital bed holding my first born, this day seemed ages away. I can recall with clarity being handed a tiny blanket-wrapped bundle of love, and thinking to myself, *"Where's the instruction manual?"*

Alas, there was no instruction manual for us that day, but that doesn't mean we weren't offered the wisdom of bystanders at each tantrum that was thrown, or each fit that was held in the hopes of getting her own way, be it candy before dinner or an adorable puppy to take home. Four and a half years later, the entire episode was repeated as I was handed yet another blanket-wrapped bundle of love. I knew at that moment that our family was complete.

"We did it, Steve," I exclaimed to my husband,

watching as he wiped tears from his eyes. I can't imagine anyone ever getting tired of this miracle.

"Another girl, I'm so happy!" he said as he bent his head to place a kiss on each of our foreheads.

Our eldest was shopping with my parents at the moment she became a big sister. As we awaited their arrival at the hospital, we marveled at how absolutely perfect this newest addition to our family was.

"God is so good to bless us with two perfect daughters." I mused. It really wasn't the fact that we had two healthy children; I was simply amazed that God allowed us to have these two specimens of perfection. To nurture and raise them the best way we see fit, into the young accomplished adults that we hope they will become.

Looking back over the past 24 and 20 years, I know I wasn't the perfect mother. Nor was Steve the perfect father. We tried our best, and I admit that we feel as though we have managed the task rather well. Our eldest is beginning a master's program in Chemistry this fall, after having turned down several internship positions at very prestigious universities. Sloan is an entering freshman at a local university, with an intent on a career in nursing.

They have made great decisions in their lives up to this point, and I don't see anything changing that. We have been blessed with daughters that are self-assured, intelligent, friendly, kind, beautiful, and blessed with many admirable qualities.

We have fulfilled our duties as parents, but hopefully will remain in their lives for years to come. Thinking back, I remembered the hours we spent with each pregnancy, choosing names that would fit a newborn, yet be substantial enough to carry these babies into adulthood.

We chose the name Hunter Ann for our first daughter. What? You may be questioning our selection of such a masculine name for an 8 lb., 4 oz. little girl, but she has lived up to the name entirely on her own. We haven't regretted it once. She says that her name was never a source of teasing from other children at school, although she did get a few raised eyebrows from the new teachers at her school.

Hunter was my mother's maiden name, and it means a lot to me. I grew up only two miles from my grandparent's home, and saw them nearly every day of my childhood. It wasn't until my grandfather passed away in 1989 that I actually came to the realization that my grandparents were such a vital part of my childhood. Even today my eyes get misty when I speak of them, and I remember them with fondness. That is one reason I wanted the Hunter name to be carried on for future generations. She has stood up to the name, carrying it well, and making us proud.

We didn't stop at just one family name for our second daughter. She got two family names. Lily Sloan completed our family in July 1997. Her name is also family oriented. Sloan was my great aunt's middle name, and Steve and I each have a great-grandmother named Lily. The only problem I have had with her name is the fact that although legally, her first name is Lily, she answers to Sloan. That fact alone is the cause for confusion at many places, such as schools, camps, library cards, and hospitals as well as doctor's offices and voter registrations. I recall the day we announced her name to the family. Both grandmothers were standing by my bed, admiring the newborn.

"What are you going to name her?" my mother in law asked, echoed by the baby's older sister, "Yeah, what's her name?" Hunter said while studying the newborn's pink and wrinkled skin.

The room grew silent as everyone awaited the proclamation of our daughter's name. I nodded my head to Steve, and he announced, "Her name is Lily Sloan," which was followed by murmurs of contentment from everyone in the room.

"But we will call her Sloan," I interjected, "because L's are difficult for me to pronounce with my MS." At that time, my pronouncement of Lily sounded more like Llullly, and I wasn't about to subject our daughter to a name even I couldn't pronounce correctly!

That day was almost 20 years ago, but it seems like only yesterday. Each of our daughters has developed into a young woman that any parent would be proud to call their own. Neither has caused my husband or me any major heartbreak. Sure, tears have been shed for various reasons, as each of us has had to experience growing pains. It seems all parents wait for their baby's first trembling steps, only to want to scoop the now-walking toddler in our arms ever so tightly.

Growing pains aren't necessarily a physical pain caused by some non-determinate injury as our children grow. Instead, I think of it as a general pain experienced by many parents as the infant they welcomed into the family grows daily. One day you are breast-feeding your little angel, and the next you are watching her flip her bangs out of her eyes as she talks with friends about the latest craze overtaking their teenage mindset. One day you prepare a fully-equipped diaper bag for a day running errands with a little one in tow, and before you realize it you are sitting in your car, looking at a gas tank indicator on E because your teen borrowed it without replenishing the gas.

I have noticed changes in the music selection for the car, too. What once started out as Barney's voice on the car stereo, singing, "I love you, you love me..." has now become the deafening clash of musical instruments, drums, and screaming vocals of the latest rock band to take the airwaves by storm. *Do kids today really call what they listen to, music?!* Some days I actually yearn for the Beatles, The Rolling Stones, and KISS. Now those were bands, not a group of prepubescent teens trying to harmonize their heartaches across the radio to thousands of love-struck 'tweens drooling over the latest fan page on the internet.

Yes, growing pains come often, not one less painful as the last. That first day of school photo that is cherished so much becomes a moment frozen in time in a scrapbook. As do the endless report cards and certificates of achievement that are tucked away in a box or drawer somewhere in your home, but you're not exactly sure where. All of these remind us of the growing pains each memory holds for us. As my husband and I turn the corner and become empty nesters this fall, there is not one single memory that I would trade for any amount of money in the world. We may not be rich, but our hearts are bursting at the seams, filled with the love and memories of two very special little girls that will always and forever have a place in our hearts, no matter how old they become.

WHAT IS STRENGTH?

I f you have ever been fortunate enough to watch a butterfly emerge from her cocoon, then you have been blessed to watch one of God's greatest miracles. To casual observers, the butterfly struggles enormously to free itself of the dark walls of the chrysalis for weeks. Once the butterfly has emerged, she must then rest while allowing her newly formed wings to dry before taking her first hesitant flight into the big beautiful world of which she is a part. Sometimes, when observers see the struggle the insect is making, that person may feel inclined to assist the butterfly and help to remove part of the cocoon from her body.

As much as we think we may be helping her to escape the dark den whereby God performed a miracle of transforming a lowly caterpillar into a gorgeous butterfly to make the world just a tiny bit more beautiful, we actually are harming the creature. However, I believe that God arranged nature so that the struggles the butterfly has when first attempting to emerge from her cocoon are actually not struggles at all. I believe that God *allows* the butterfly to struggle in order for her to exercise her wings so that she will be strong enough to handle herself outside of her cocoon, no matter what dangers there may be.

That is the same way God helps us through our own dark and depressing times. He allows us to struggle so that we will become stronger in the long run.

I'll admit that there have been many times that my MS has seemed like a burden rather than a struggle. Especially now, it really seems as though I can't catch a break health-wise.

Last week I underwent my second lumpectomy in 14 months. I have an appointment in two days with my surgeon. At this appointment, I will get the news as to whether the lump was malignant or benign, and find out what type of treatment my doctor recommends. As hard as I try to think of my struggles as exercises for my body and mind to help me carry on with the rest of my life, it's hard for me to see them that way.

We each should take the struggles in our lives and view them as challenges. It is not always an easy thing to do, but I believe God allows these things to happen to us for reasons only He knows, and we will discover those reasons some day when we stand before Him in Heavenly Glory.

After everything that I have been through medically in the past two years alone, I try to see each new diagnosis as another platform on which I can reach out to others. I learn as much as I possibly can about each new ailment, and then proceed to teach others about it, either online in group chats, or when I'm talking to the people in public. It makes the diagnosis a little easier for me to bear, and

I hope that by educating others, it may make someone's diagnosis a little easier to accept.

I know that God already knows what will happen in my life, and He will be here to help me get through it. That is one reason I have no fear or trepidation waiting for my next appointment. God is good, and He is my strength and my shield. I'm not saying that I am ready to join God in His kingdom, because I hope that I have several years left here on this Earth. I want to hold in my arms at least one grandchild before I leave.

I will admit that I have decided which two Hymns I would like to be sung at my funeral, no matter when that is going to take place. I want *"How Great Thou Art"* and *"Morning Has Broken"* to be played loudly as family and friends gather to say their goodbyes to me. I want the words to be shouted as well as sung, so that the angels will hear them, and know that I am taking my place beside them in God's presence.

This may seem rather morbid to you, but I have honestly been thinking about these things since 2014, when I lapsed into unconsciousness for 10 days while battling a diseased gall bladder, Septicemia, kidney stones, and breast cancer. I don't think it is morbid at all to request a few things for your own funeral. I'm not planning the entire thing! I know I am someone who doesn't like to give up control of the situation at times, but as long as I have these two hymns played and my favorite verse read (Isaiah 40:31), I promise not to haunt anyone.

Tips for people with MS: How to Minimize the Ripple

Multiple sclerosis is not an easy disease to live with. I guess if it were pleasant, it wouldn't be considered a disease! Here is a chapter filled with tips, advice, and a few suggestions on how to make MS a part of your life without it *becoming* your life. I only wish that I could have read these things, and taken them to heart, when I was first diagnosed with this disease that has become a major part of who I am.

Every person with the Multiple Sclerosis diagnosis is different, so not all of the points covered in this chapter will apply to each person. Instead, I am offering this chapter as a chapter of hope, and not filled with details of how terrible this disease can be.

I can still recall the first visit to my neurologist in 1986. My mom and I sat across from his desk while he explained Multiple Sclerosis to us. He told us that researchers were working on possible cures at a high rate, and hopefully, a cure for MS is just months away. That gave me hope that day, just knowing that there were people in labs across the world looking for a cure.

The very next thing he told me was that I needed to lose as much weight as possible to make it easier to walk, etc. At that time in my life, I never imagined myself not being able to walk, so I never really tried that hard to lose weight. I was 5'9" and weighed approximately 170 pounds. I knew I should lose weight, but didn't. Today, I weigh about 150 and can tell just how much easier it is for people to help me. I wish that I had been smart enough to get in better shape in 1986, but hindsight definitely is 20/20!

Needless to say, it is now 2017 and the fact there still is no cure is a testament to just how difficult it is to find cures for things. I haven't lost hope, but I am encouraged because in 1986 there were no available medications for MS, and today there are numerous medications available to deal with the exacerbations of MS as well as a plethora of medications to help deal with various symptoms.

In 1986, the most promising drug was Prednisone, which brings so many side-effects with it I can't even remember them all. I remember asking for more Prednisone each time I felt an exacerbation come along. I hated how it made me feel, but each time after a few weeks of Prednisone, I would be back to my almost pre-MS self for a while, albeit a few pounds heavier.

Another thing that I wish I had done was stretching to keep my muscles limber. Flexibility has gone out the window over the course of many exacerbations and age. I really regret not keeping up with stretching my muscles more. Some of the rigidity in my leg muscles is quite severe, and I like to think that if I had kept up a routine of stretching it might not be as bad.

My dad has sat with me for hours at a time helping to relieve some of the spasticity in my legs. My husband and daughters try to help me stretch also, but I think my dad does it best because he knows it hurts, but he also knows it is necessary to cause a little pain to reclaim some flexibility. I'm not saying Steve and the girls don't know the importance of stretching, but I know it pains them terribly to hear my grunts and whimpers over the course of a therapy session.

For years, I prided myself with household chores such as laundry, cooking, and cleaning. I will never be an immaculate housekeeper, but I kept my apartments tidy. In 2001, I thought that it would be better for me to get an electric wheelchair. It seemed to help me with the daily chores around the house at first. It enabled me to take a load of clothes out of the dryer in the laundry room, sit on the couch to fold them, and ultimately take the stacks of clean clothes to its destination, which was something I was finding increasingly difficult to do while in a manual wheelchair.

I could collect dirty dishes from around the house (for example) and take them to the kitchen with ease, whereas I needed both arms to push myself around in a manual chair. My intention upon getting my first electric wheelchair was to use it only when it was necessary in tidying up the house, carrying things, or my MS was in an exacerbation.

Very quickly, I was using the power chair all the time. I now regret getting a power wheelchair as early as I did.

Yes, it made things easier for me in the short term, but the more I used it, the more comfortable I became with it, and the more dependent I was on it. I would even take my electric chair outdoors to water plants; fill the bird feeders, etc.

A few times I even got myself in trouble by getting stuck in mud, in a tight space, or even just by falling out of the chair while outdoors! Luckily, my family is nearby to help me get out of these messes. As a precaution, I resorted to carrying my cell phone in a pouch around my neck. Believe me when I say that has saved me from many dire situations!

Just as important as keeping flexible is not letting your mental state slide downhill as a result of being disabled. Crossword puzzles, Sudoku, word searches, and mental brain teasers are all excellent ways to stay mentally sharp while my body stays in place fighting MS. Reading in general also helps me to remain focused on the outside world, and not keep to myself- which almost always leads to feeling sorry for myself!

I'll admit that on some days I *do* feel sorry for myself, but I make the effort not to allow those feelings to hang around very long. Prayer always helps me immensely when these feelings start to overtake my usually positive mind set. I wish that I had a secret formula for getting over the feelings of self-pity, but I don't.

Every person has within themselves the power to overcome such negative feelings. I have been taking antidepressants for years now, and my family makes sure I don't run out! Sometimes just being outdoors helps me to see my situation in a different perspective. I figure that as bad as my situation is at any given time, someone somewhere is battling their own demons- and their situation is probably worse than mine!

After being diagnosed, I attended a support groups for MS patients and their families/friends in the Dallas area. Instead of giving me hope for a better future, I came away in a state of shock. Until I had attended the support group, I was aware that permanent disability was a possibility, but actually seeing a group of people with wheelchairs, walkers, canes, etc. brought me to the painful realization that the same things were most likely in my future, and it scared me! I'm ashamed now to admit that I dealt with this realization by blocking it from memory.

I sometimes wish that I had given the group another try, but instead I thanked them for allowing me to spend time with the group, but told them this just wasn't for me. I'm ashamed that I even had those thoughts, much less spoke them aloud to these wonderful people. I was still in a state of denial over the diagnosis, and I just knew that I would be the one person to conquer all the stereotypes. A member of the group said it best when he said,

"You're not ready for this group yet, but we will still be here for you when you're ready to come back."

Those words still haunt me. A perfect stranger knew more about my mental state than I did! I never went to the support group again, but it would have been helpful to me in accepting life's changes as my MS progressed. I often wonder how the people I met that evening are doing. I could have made some very good friends in that group, had I just given them the chance. I thought that I was strong enough to handle all aspects of MS by myself, but now I realize that no one can be that strong.

We all need the love and support of our families and friends, in whatever form it comes. Whatever you do, don't try to fight this battle on your own. MS is a strength-draining disease, and each person needs all the strength they can muster to fight the way out of the mind-numbing array of neurological tests, MRIs, doctors, physical therapists, and neurologists that will most probably be in your future.

One thing that has helped me not to feel victimized is knowledge. This is a very important thing to many people with MS and other similar diseases, because feeling like a victim is equivalent to pity and this is the last thing that many with these types of illness even want from others.

Once you realize that are going to spend possibly the rest of your life in a wheelchair or walker or even with a cane you need to find ways to get people to respect you and not pity you. When you greet people make sure to get their attention in some way with your eyes as this will prevent them from staring at your chair, legs, or walker. It makes a difference when you can meet their gaze with your own. I read about the current research that is being performed world-wide by researching online, reading the monthly National Multiple Sclerosis Society (NMSS) publications, and even staying abreast of local research here in Arkansas. I feel that this empowers me somewhat by knowing the research that is going on. It also makes me feel as though I am part of a community of people with MS who are not taking this diagnosis lying down! Or in my case, sitting down!

I guess the most important thing I have learned over the years is to ask for help when it's needed. Never discredit the people who truly love and care for you. People in general are more than happy to lend assistance if it is asked for in a sincere, polite way, and with a grateful heart. And always, always keep your line of communication open to a being with a higher power, no matter your chosen denomination.

Your MS journey will not be the same as any other MS journey, because this disease is as individualistic as the patients diagnosed with it. This means that each person living with this disease is given the opportunity to make their lives meaningful, in whichever way they see fit.

You may be one person in the midst of thousands living with this disease, but it is up to you to see how you fit into the scheme of things, and make sure that your life has a purpose to it, in whichever ways you choose to use it.

BECOMING A STUDENT ONCE AGAIN

If there is one thing that I credit for getting me off the couch, and away from being in front of the television, I would have to say it is online education. Yes, I received my Bachelor of Arts degree in Communication with an emphasis on marketing and public relations back in 1986. I'm proud of that degree, although I never became the powerful public relations executive that I once dreamed of becoming. At least that is what I thought I wanted in my teen years. My very first post-college job came to me simply because I wanted to live in Dallas.

I filled the position of account representative at a large insurance firm in Dallas, where I was assigned 5 districts in Texas to follow up on the monthly renewals, claims, etc. and hopefully try to retain the business upon their renewal each year. Each month I was responsible for anywhere from fifty to 250 insurer's policies and the salesmen and women in each district office.

By 2010, after we had moved back to my hometown, I was beginning to get a little bored with being a stay-at-home mom to the kids. We had lived here for about ten years and the girls were getting older. My MS was pretty much manageable at this time, the girls were in school each day, Steve attended a local university to receive his Bachelor's and then his Master's degrees, and I stayed home, washed clothes, cleaned bathrooms, the kitchen, and basically spent the days watching television.

Let me tell you that it doesn't matter how many channels you get on your television set, there is really nothing of great importance on daytime television. Our satellite server offers many channels, but I found myself tuning into CNN or watching reruns of 1970's shows most often. Then, when the kids came home from school it would be time for homework and family time until dinner. My life was predictably boring.

One night as the girls got ready for bed, Steve asked me if I was happy. "Of course I'm happy, babe," I said to him. "We are raising the kids in the same way I was raised, I have lots of family living nearby, and why wouldn't I be happy?" I didn't realize it at the time, but I was trying to persuade myself that I had everything I could want. "Why do you ask?"

"I don't know, you just seem unhappy these days," he commented before returning to his book. That question and his response to my answer lingered on my mind the rest of the week. When the weekend rolled around, I broached the subject to him.

"Remember last week when you asked if I was happy," I questioned.

"Yeah. So now you're not happy?" Steve turned in this

chair to face me. "What's up, Nan? Are you un happy here? What can I do to help you?"

"I don't really know what it is; I mean we're living in our own house, on a piece of property I've always admired, raising our kids in the country. It's what I always wished for..." my voice trailed off as I finished talking. I brushed the hair out of my eyes as Steve held my gaze, his eyes questioning me.

"Well, I hate to say this, but I feel jealous of you," I reluctantly started. "I'm jealous that you get to go to your classes and have adult conversations," I raised my head.

"We don't really have conversations about anything except class-related things," Steve replied. "I'll do whatever I need to do to make you happy, Nan," he said with a hint of resignation in his voice. "Just tell me what I can do for you."

"I don't know, Steve," I said. "It's probably just me. The girls are growing up, and I'm not quite ready to be a grandmother yet." At this time, Hunter walked into the room and stopped, glancing between us with a puzzled look.

"What?" She practically screamed to us, "Grandmother?? Who, what, tell me what you're saying!?"

Steve and I both laughed at her reaction before he said, "Relax, we both know what you've always told us. You don't want kids of your own," Steve gave her a reassuring hug. By now it was time for dinner, so we made our way to the kitchen where we ate at the bar.

After dinner, I mentioned to Steve that I may want to take a class at one of the local universities next semester.

"I think that would be great," he exclaimed. "I think

you would love it," he continued. "What class do you think you would want to take?" That question opened a lot of possibilities, and I wasn't even sure that I could take a class with my MS sometimes keeping me in bed until noon. That night I fell asleep with pictures of myself, in a wheelchair, making my way across campus, possibly being late to class because my wheelchair tire had gotten stuck. I wasn't sure I liked that picture or not, so I placed it in the back of my mind.

The week passed with no further discussion of the topic. The following weekend Steve sat at the computer in our den while I folded laundry, stacking the clothes according to which room they belonged. The television was on and Sloan was giving her dog a much-needed bath in the girls' bathroom. We could hear squeals amid her authoritative commands telling Walt,

"Sit, be still," and "No don't shake yet!" coming from the bathroom to where we were sitting in the den. Steve turned from his computer and said,

"Nan, come look at this for a minute." This surprised me because I was expecting him to tell me to ask Sloan to wash the dog without yelling.

I moved my chair closer to his and looked at the computer screen; it was a welcome screen to a university's home page. Southern New Hampshire University as a matter of fact.

"What's that, are we moving to New Hampshire?" I asked. "No," he said. "But they have an online creative writing degree, and I thought you may be interested in it."

Well, that caught my attention right way! Steve went

to rescue either Walt or Sloan, or both from the bubbles and bath.

I sat at the computer until the wet dog smell permeated my thoughts. Steve and Sloan had finished giving Walt his bath and had rewarded him by letting him come to the den to show me just how clean he was. *I have always wanted to write a book*, I thought. *Maybe a Master's degree in Creative Writing will help.* I thought to myself. *It can't hurt to look into it.*

Continuing my education was the perfect solution to my lackluster days, it turned out. Through my courses, I have met so many different types of people that I cannot imagine my life without them in it. I am in contact with them daily through Facebook. I've supported them through deaths in their families, weddings, and births, as well as offered encouragement and prayers for their daily struggles and their blessings.

In many ways, I feel closer to them than I feel towards my "in-person" friends. They have been with me through their divorces as well as weddings, abusive relationships and good relationships, the publishing of their first book, as well as the hundreds of rejection letters that are sure to find their ways to each of us.

It isn't only the friendships that I value so much, but the added value this accomplishment has given me is hard to measure. Each day, before I even have my coffee, I stop at my computer to check in with my classes. I'll admit that I am having a harder time adjusting to my new classes in my quest for a second Master's degree. I'm not sure what the difference is in these two departments, maybe the students are younger, and just want to do enough to get a passing grade, or maybe these students are not as passionate about their marketing courses as we were in the Creative Writing courses. I'm about to begin my third-to-last class towards my Master of Science degree, and I'm hoping to make some more good friends along the way.

Either way, I know that online education is so worth the expense and time that it consumes. It has broadened my horizons so much that I can't imagine what my life would be like without these bridges I am crossing, and I am so grateful that these bridges are there for me to venture across. I'm thankful for the advent of online education, not just for me, but there are so many others that can broaden their horizons in this way.

I happen to be in a wheelchair, so an online program suited my lifestyle ideally. At first I was worried about the technology involved in becoming an online student, but that has turned out to be nothing to worry about. I am proud to be a graduate of an online program, and feel that the fact it is an online program does not diminish the value of the degree one bit. I am proud to be able to place the initials BA, MA, and MS after my name!

LIKE IT OR NOT, IT'S BACK

"It's back," I announced unceremoniously to Steve one Friday night in August 2015. We had just returned from an evening out of town, and both of us were weary of all the things that were happening in our lives at the moment.

"What's back?" Steve asked apprehensively as I continued to undress.

"A lump. Here, in my breast," I told him. I wasn't worried, I had been wearing a new bra and I hadn't noticed how uncomfortable it was until I took it off. I continued palpating my breast as Steve walked toward me. "I think it was my bra," I said, hoping to dismiss the entire thing and get some much-needed rest.

"Let me see, Nan," Steve said as he walked toward the bed where I was already snuggling under the covers.

I dutifully raised my right arm above my head and showed him the lump I had felt moments earlier.

"That's an insect bite," Steve exclaimed with relief.

I sat up in bed, "Oh, I guess it is," I agreed somewhat sheepishly, laughing.

"Either a bug bite, or my bra pinched me." I laughed with relief as I lay my head on the pillow.

We both put the lump out of our minds for a night of restful sleep. This time of year seemed busier to me in some ways. I had received my Master of Arts degree in English and Creative Writing from Southern New Hampshire's online degree program a few weeks earlier, an accomplishment for which I was proud. Steve was preparing to take his exams for his doctorate in Education, Hunter was beginning a graduate program in Environmental Chemistry at the University of Arkansas at Little Rock, and Sloan was beginning her college career at Henderson State University here in town.

In the meantime, I had decided to pursue yet another Master's degree from SNHU- this time in marketing. I didn't like the feeling of having nothing productive to do, so why not pursue another degree? Steve supported me in this endeavor, and even said he would help me in some of the business classes if I needed it. Our lives were set for the next year.

The next morning, my eyes flew open around seven o'clock. My mind immediately went to the insect bite. It was still there. In fact, if I thought about it, it felt oddly familiar. It felt very similar to the lump I'd had removed from my right breast 14 months earlier, only it didn't. This time the lump was more toward the surface of my skin, almost to my armpit, whereas last year's lump was deep within the breast tissue. It was large enough to be visible to the naked eye. *What does this mean?* I wondered. My mind raced to the scene in the movie *Terms of Endearment*, where Shirley McClain was discussing Debra Winger's breast lump, and she said,

"It's probably a clogged duct or something; you never have been very good about cleaning yourself." *Oh, how I hope and pray that will be the case with my lump!* Especially when I allow myself to think more about the movie. Debra Winger's goodbye scene with her oldest child brings tears to my eyes when I just think of her saying, "You don't have to like me." I tear up remembering that scene every time.

But that's not me, I tell myself. I know in my heart that I did not come close to death last year, only to recover from my surgeries and to finish writing my book that I have wanted to write for nearly 31 years now, find a publisher, complete one graduate degree and start on another one, to simply give up on life and succumb to cancer!

I have seen the other side, have felt the warmth radiating from the brightest light you can imagine, have seen so many brilliant and vibrant colors for which there are no names, I have felt absolute happiness in my soul which words cannot describe. I know there is an afterlife waiting for me, but as wonderful as it is, I am in no rush to attain the heights promised me by my Lord. I recall the terrible sense of sadness and despair when I was told to return to Earth because my daughters need me. It was not a pleasing sensation, to be told I could not stay in His Heavenly kingdom.

Once the weekend was over, I concentrated on finding a doctor, getting an appointment for a mammogram, and getting my records from last year's mammogram transferred to my new doctor. Steve and I had decided that it would be best for me if all my doctors were located at the University of Arkansas for Medical Science Center in Little Rock. That is where my neurologist has his office, and we discovered while I was hospitalized last year, that although the doctors caring or me were good, they had no desire to include my neurologist in on any discussions regarding my health simply because he didn't have privileges at the hospital I was taken to in an unconscious state last year.

We figure that if anything even similar to the same thing happens again, it would be best to have all of my doctors centrally located, in one hospital.

My appointment for the mammogram was scheduled for Tuesday. Going to the State hospital was a far cry from my experiences at the hospital last year. For example, the waiting room for my mammogram was tiny, crowded, with publications from three years ago to read while waiting, and didn't even have a window to the outdoors! It was loud, also. The phone kept ringing behind the desk, and the over-worked receptionist seemed to be speaking loudly into the receiver. I assumed this was the same person I had contacted for my appointment. I recall having to spell my last name for her several times during my initial call.

My first instincts were to turn around and go to my previous hospital. I longed for the quiet, carpeted halls, large waiting rooms with comfortable upholstered chairs, with fresh paint on the walls and fresh flowers in vases. Steve caught my eye, and asked if I wanted to leave. I silently shook my head in the negative in response to his question. We were already here, so why would I leave? Sure the other hospital was more aesthetically pleasing, with touches of comfort that mimicked home, but I am not here to evaluate the décor, I'm here to address this lump in my breast! I was called to the back for the mammogram 30 minutes later.

Once I was in the "holding cell" for my turn at the mammography, I had to laugh to myself. I was placed in a closet with a curtain for a door. When I tell you it was small, I'm not exaggerating the fact that I couldn't even straighten my arms fully and I was touching both walls! In fact my elbows remained bent at an almost 90-degree angle! *No, Nancy you are not at a private hospital anymore!*

Nonetheless, the nurses were kind, personable, and talked me through each step. The mammogram itself was nothing new, just a lot of tugging and pushing to get the best angle. I simply turned my head and let the nurses tug, push, and pull on my breasts while the machine squeezed them to what felt like a quarter of an inch thick. I then would hold perfectly still until the pain almost caused me to pass out, when suddenly the whirring of the machine stopped and my breast was released from the medieval torture chamber. I was taken back to my "closet" to wait for an ultrasound of the lump to be performed.

The ultrasound was so much more pleasant. The technician even had warmed gel to use during the procedure. After the ultrasound, a radiologist came to speak to me, Steve, and Hunter. He said that I needed to have a biopsy performed on the lump. After the biopsy, it will be known as malignant or not, and my doctor will help me decide on a course of action. I have an appointment scheduled for one week from today, and hopefully the doctor can perform the biopsy that day. So here I am in limbo once again. Waiting for test results, which will determine if I have cancer or not. All I can do is stay positive, and pray. I don't think my inner self can stay positive, but at least I prayed.

I prayed that God would take me quickly, if it was my time to join him. That part really didn't scare me, because I knew deep within my soul that I have a place in heaven waiting for me. I prayed that my illness would not affect my family too much, that Sloan would not let my illness deter her from completing a nursing degree or whatever type of degree she wants to pursue. I prayed that Hunter will continue to excel in her pursuit of a career in Environmental Chemistry, and that my illness will not cause too many complications in her life.

I prayed that Steve will finally achieve his dream of teaching students at the higher education level, and that he would be successful in his career. I prayed that my parents would not worry about me excessively, and that they will continue to enjoy their new home and retirement with the assurance that they have given me an amazing life, and I have no regrets. Lastly, I prayed that my nieces and nephews who are grown now, would remember me to their children with fondness, and not as the sickly relative in the wheelchair.

The next seven days seemed to drag on and on, much like the days before Christmas when I was a child. Each night as I crawled into bed, I would feel for the lump in my breast. It must have been my imagination, but I could have sworn the lump was getting larger each time I felt it. Steve tried to reassure me that it wasn't getting larger; it was just my fears that were growing.

Finally, the seven days passed and we were on our way to surgery. The waiting room was cramped, but we managed to find two adjoining seats where Steve placed his bag full of study materials beside him before slumping into a seat with a fresh cup of coffee. I was called into pre-op relatively quickly, so I didn't have much time to get nervous. I can't say the same for Steve, as I recalled him being up most of the night before. I hadn't been able to sleep very well, either. I gave his hand a squeeze as the nurse took me to the operating room.

Once there, I was led to a bed at the end of a row of similar beds. I noticed my name was handwritten on a board that was at the foot of my bed. *Wayland, N. Well, I guess this is really happening,* I thought as the nurses put the different colored arm bands on my wrist. A white one with all the important information on it such as my name, date of birth, my doctor's name, etc. was placed on my wrist first, then two other ones.

A bright yellow one announced to everyone that I was a fall risk, which I found to be slightly humorous, because I can't even stand alone, then an orange bracelet that announced my allergy to Dexamethazone, which is a steroid that causes hives if I take it. The reaction of hives seems like such a trivial thing to me, I don't think it deserves its own bracelet. *Who cares about hives when the stake is so much larger, such as breast cancer?*

I was wheeled into the operating room, where my surgeon greeted me before turning to gown up for surgery. The next thing I remember, I heard a loud voice telling me to wake up, and that the surgery was over. I have been under anesthesia over a dozen times in the past year, but it never fails to surprise me how time seems to stand still while I am under the effects of anesthesia. To me, it felt as though I had just been wheeled into surgery, and now they were telling me to wake up? It wasn't until the nurse offered me some ginger ale that I finally realized it was over. I swallowed the ginger ale as though I had been walking through a desert, I was so thirsty. After an hour in recovery, Steve helped me dress and we were free to go home.

We saw my surgeon, and the nurse made me an appointment for the next week, then Steve and I were on our way home. We both felt as though a very heavy weight had been lifted from our shoulders, even though it would be another seven days before we knew if it was malignant or not. Either way, Dr. Klemming was certain that I would be needing radiation treatments. We will know more about this following another seven days of limbo. So again, we wait. And again, the week dragged by as though it were the week before Christmas!

When we arrived at Dr. Klemming's office once again, the surgeon told me that although she was sure she had removed all the cancerous cells, she still wanted to have the cells tested further.

"I've been told once before that all of the cancerous cells were removed after my lumpectomy last year," I stated, "so you will forgive me if I take your news with a grain of salt."

"Oh, certainly," Dr. Klemming answered. "I wouldn't expect anything less from a patient."

Steve and I sat quietly in the exam room, listening intently. I wondered what was going through his mind. *He agreed to marry me 23 years ago, despite my MS diagnosis, but I'm sure he never anticipated breast cancer to be a part of the equation, too!*

I felt as though I had received good news as we left the office. In fact, the closer we got to home, the better I felt.

"I'm sorry, babe," I said as Steve turned his truck into our driveway.

"About what, Nan?" he asked.

"Well I know you weren't prepared to deal with cancer again so soon after my hospitalization last summer."

"Nan, you know I'll always be here for you, I just wish all of this wasn't happening at the same time as my qualifying exams, but it is."

"I know, and I'll help you do whatever you need me to do to help." Steve smiled wryly as he handed me a stack of papers. He had been studying for these exams off and on for months, so the papers were a little wrinkled, as well as showing the remains of spilled coffee stains. I attempted to smooth the pages the best I could before quizzing him.

Later that week, I answered the phone and was surprised to hear Dr. Klemming's voice on the other end.

"This is Dr. Klemming from UAMS," she began. I was still in bed at ten o'clock that morning, but just hearing her voice caused me to sit upright in bed. Steve happened to be walking through the room, and stopped to look at me when I sat up. He reached for the remote control to turn off the television, which just happened to be showing a commercial for the Susan G. Koeman Race for the Cure that is to be held in Little Rock soon.

"Yes, Dr. Klemming, this is Nancy," I said while I

wondered if she could hear my heart beating through the telephone line.

"Nancy, I'm sorry to tell you that the cells I sent for further testing came back positive. That means they were malignant." She didn't have to tell me positive equaled malignant, but I guess she said that to make sure I was clear on the matter.

"Oh, I see," I replied automatically. "What is the next step in treatment?" As Dr. Klemming was answering my question, I handed the phone to Steve. I couldn't breathe at this point, silently, tears began flowing from my eyes.

"Okay, Dr. Klemming," Steve said into the phone while placing his arm around my shoulders. "Will your office be making the appointment for us with the Oncologist?" and after a few more pleasantries, he hung up the phone before enveloping me in his arms.

Although I was crying, I was not sobbing. I knew that for some reason I have been given yet another burden to bear. I don't know why, and won't know until I am in God's presence someday, the best thing I can do is to face the consequences the best I am able. I pray that radiation and chemotherapy can kill the cancer cells within me, but if not, I will try my best to be an advocate for early detection. It was difficult for me to tell my parents. Mom cried when I told her.

"You just can't seem to get a break," she said, between sobs.

"Mom, I'll be fine. We will make it through this," I said quickly, before I lost control of the tears I was struggling to choke back. "I'll talk to you later."

When mom and I talked later that night, she seemed

resigned to the diagnosis. I had to keep reminding myself that my body was a walking time bomb, with potentially cancerous cells spreading through my body at will. My next appointment was with an Oncologist. *Would the drives to Little Rock ever come to an end?*

Steve and I met with Dr. Medford his office the following week. Now Dr. Medford wanted to send my breast tissue to California for a specific test to see if some levels of something was above 51% or not. If the percentages were of this certain hormone or something were below 51%, I could just get by with 5 weeks of radiation. However, if the percentage of this certain thing was above 51%, Chemotherapy would also be required.

"Of course," Dr. Medford said, "a double Mastectomy is always an option for women in this instance."

I nodded my head, and said, "I'm for that if it would take away my risks for developing breast cancer!" I am ready to have my breasts removed. *After all, they have served me well for 51 years, I have nourished my children with them and even flaunted them a bit when I was younger, if removing them from my body could remove the risk of another return of breast cancer, why shouldn't I?*

Steve held his hand up as if to stop the forward progress of the conversation.

"Well, Nan, we'll see about this. The results will be back ...?" and he looked to Dr. Medford for the answer.

"The tests will take about 4 weeks to come in," the doctor replied. "In the meantime, the two of you can discuss the mastectomy issue further."

So that is where we stand now, waiting another 3 ½ weeks for results. At least I should know the answer before

Thanksgiving. So now, once again, we are waiting, and praying for some clear results to come through. *Why, oh why, does time pass so slowly just when you don't want it to, and seem to fly by at other times, like when your children are young?*

One night two weeks later, Sloan was helping me get changed for bed after the three of us had spent the day in Hot Springs. she looked at my right thigh, which was bulging outward quite a bit, and was extremely warm to the touch.

"Oh my gosh, Dad, come in here," Sloan called to Steve in the next room. "Look at mom's leg!"

Steve came in the room, saw my leg, and announced, "Get back in the van, we're going to the hospital."

After some initial resisting from me, we all got back in the van and headed to the local emergency room. Once there, the doctor on call looked at my leg, determined it may be a Deep Vein Thrombosis and then told us that the Emergency Room didn't have access to a working ultrasound at the moment, and I would need to go to another hospital for an ultrasound and diagnosis.

We were incredulous. *He was telling me to go to another hospital in another town to get diagnosed?* We ended up going home that night, and travelled to Hot Springs the following morning. Once we were in the hospital emergency room in Hot Springs, the doctors and nurses could not believe the fact that we had been in an ER the night before and had been sent back home.

"Do you mean to tell me that the doctor there looked at your leg, mentioned it may be a DVT, and then sent you home without blood thinners or anything?" the doctor asked, then simply shook his head slowly as I answered in the affirmative. The doctor seemed to be finding my version of events rather hard to believe.

"This DVT could have broken loose while you were moving around, and you probably wouldn't even be here today."

With that, and knowing my history with blood clots in my lungs a year earlier, the doctor prescribed Eliquis for me, to be taken daily for the rest of my life. I didn't even think this would factor into my decision for a double mastectomy, but found out it was in fact, a major development.

We went to my doctor's appointment two weeks later to tell him of my decision to have a double mastectomy. I was anxious to get this surgery behind me. When Dr. Medford entered the exam room, I informed him of the DVT experience two weeks before.

"You had a DVT recently?" he sounded surprised.

"Yes, I did, but it has been dissolved now," I said while indicating on my thigh where it had been. "I'm on blood thinners for life, now."

He excused himself and came back a few minutes later. "I am unwilling to perform the double mastectomy on you now that you've had two pulmonary embolisms and now this recent DVT."

My face was crestfallen as I realized the double mastectomy was no longer an option. I looked at Steve, he looked relieved that this meant one less surgery in my future, but neither of us had any idea of what was to come. I got over my disappointment over my breasts not being removed. I had actually been looking forward to not wearing a bra anymore, especially in the summers, but I will just continue wearing bras and getting my mammograms annually as usual.

The following weeks found me travelling to Hot Springs on a daily basis for radiation treatments, for 5 weeks. I met many wonderful people on my journey through the medical establishments in Arkadelphia, Hot Springs, and Little Rock. Not any one person was less amazing than the next. Though there were days when I was so exhausted from the effects of the radiation, I made it through each and every treatment as was necessary.

I feel that my daughters now must face the increased likelihood of being diagnosed with Multiple Sclerosis, but also Breast Cancer as well. That is a burden they bear just by being born to me. I hope that I have shown them an example of how to handle these life-altering events with grace and thankfulness.

I am continually thankful for the discoveries and improvements in the medical fields, and for the caring doctors, nurses, and supporting members of the medical field. I am extremely grateful for these experiences that brought me into contact with so many amazing people who inspired and encouraged me along the way. I believe that keeping a positive attitude is essential when fighting any disease that may come your way.

Keeping your spirits up in times of distress, may at times seem impossible, but just remember that butterfly struggling to get out of its chrysalis so it can fill the world with just a small bit of beauty. Just keep your head and your spirits up, and continue struggling through whatever God has allowed to come your way, and know in your heart, your struggles are actually exercises designed to make you a better person.

ANOTHER CAUSE
FOUND *ME!*

W hile in the process of completing this book, I have had the opportunity to read over the individual essays quite a few times and cringing over every error of speech or writing, and asking myself, *"Why did I write that?"* and *"why did I write the same information over and over?"* Now that the book is finished and I can no longer adjust it, I can only answer that the reasons for the duplicate stories from one essay to another are the result of my inadequacies as an author. I spent over 3 years gathering the essays together, and my memory is not as great as it once was, and I would forget while editing one essay, what I had written in another, and so on it goes... In fact, I had originally not planned to put this final essay in the book, but I am, because the happenings in this final essay are a large part of who I am, and who our family is.

I think everyone who has a child to raise, either biologically or through adoption, or foster care, wants just one main thing in that child's life, and that is for them to be happy in life. We were faced with this head-on a couple days before Christmas 2016. Hunter had called me to ask if the three of us would be home later that day. I didn't know of any plans, so I asked Steve and Sloan if they would be home later, around early evening. They both adjusted their schedules to be home and Hunter said to me,

"I have something to tell you guys." Steve and I racked our brains the rest of the day, trying to guess what she would be telling us. Her final words before she ended the call didn't help us much, either as she had said,

"Mom, don't worry, it's not bad. It's something good."

For the remainder of the day, as Sloan worked at the restaurant, and Steve and I attempted to clean our house, do laundry, vacuum, dust, and other chores that had been put on the back burner for way too long, we kept trying to guess Hunter's news for us.

"I'll bet she's gay," one of us would say. Then a moment later the other one of us would come up with an entirely different scenario.

"She's dropping out of grad school," or "She's moving away to another state." Finally after tiring of this so-called game, I told Steve,

"It doesn't matter what she tells us, we will support her no matter what."

"Of course, we will, Nan," was Steve's prompt reply, "we will always be here for her."

Sloan came in from work and we ate dinner, then cleaned the kitchen. As we sat in the den awaiting Hunter's arrival, the guessing game began again. This time, the three of us were bouncing around the same ideas as before, as none of us had a clue what the news would be. We heard Hunter's truck in the driveway at the same time, and listened as she got out of her truck and walked across the deck to the back door. Suddenly, the door burst open with Hunter and Lolly bounding into the laundry room, through the kitchen, and into the den.

"Hey, Lolly, you're getting big aren't you," I said as the black lab mixed dog came to me for affection.

"Yeah, I don't think you have seen her in a while."

"We sure haven't," Steve replied, "but what is your news?" There's no beating around the bush for Steve. He was curious and wanted the suspense we had been feeling all day to come to an end.

The three of us waited with baited breath as Hunter took a deep breath and said,

"I am transgender."

As Steve, Sloan, and I attempted to process what Hunter had just told us, she attempted to explain how she felt,

"I have never been comfortable in my own skin and have never enjoyed dressing as a girl," she began," you know that, mom. I've been seeing a psychologist for a while now, and he's helping me to understand what's going on."

Slowly, each of us came around to the realization that we weren't watching a movie, but experiencing this in Real Life.

"I know this is a shock to all of you, and you can ask me any questions you want." After a few moments, I spoke,

"Does this mean you will be gay, lesbian, bi-sexual, or what?" In addition to trying to understand what she was telling us, I was aware of my speech, thinking back to a conversation I had with Hunter several months ago.

We had been talking on the phone, and she had asked how a high school friend was doing. I said offhandedly that I didn't know, I hadn't heard from him in a while, he must be doing his LTBG thing as usual. I didn't mean any disrespect, but said,

"LTBG or whatever they're calling it these days."

Hunter had quickly corrected me, "mom it's LBGT." I was fearful that I may have offended her by speaking the initials out of order in a flippant manner. That thought made me think there are some really rude, ignorant people in this world who don't know Hunter as we have known her the past 24 years, and immediately my eyes filled with tears.

"Mom, this has nothing to do with sex. It's about how I feel inside, and for once in my life I am truly happy with the person I am becoming. In fact, I don't really know, myself, she replied in answer to my question. "I know that I don't have feelings for females, and I still favor men, but who knows if that will change someday."

"I want everyone to understand that trans people are not perverts, or weird, and most of us have no desire to harm anyone. We are simply trying to match our external bodies with the body we have been given in our minds, I don't exactly know how to explain it to you…" Her voice trailed off as she attempted to explain what transgender means.

That wasn't really the answer I had been looking for, but this entire conversation hadn't been going as I had thought it would. At least she was honest with me on that point. Hunter was busy talking with Steve and Sloan and was unaware of the emotions I was feeling at the moment.

I am happy for her if she is happy, and it appears she truly is. She explained how she would begin Hormone Replacement Therapy in January, how her voice would lower somewhat, and she will begin growing facial hair. Then she mentioned the surgeries that would come after a few years. She will get a double mastectomy first, then get the bottom surgery after she has saved the money for it. She plans on completing her Master degree in Environmental Toxicology, then moving away to New Mexico or some other place to finish her transition before moving back home to Arkansas as an entirely different person.

"I will have to tell my professors about the transition so they won't write referrals for me saying, *she* is adept in the lab. I want to make a clean start as a male someday. Mom, do you think you will ever be able to use male pronouns when referring to me?"

I was as honest as I could be, and answered her,

"I'll try my best Hunter, but you have been my little girl for almost 24 years now. It won't be easy at first, but I promise I will try my best."

"Mom, you will still have all the memories and pictures of me as a little girl, but just realize that I'm finally happy with myself. I have never liked the person I saw when I looked in the mirror, and now I will."

We talked about how this was going to change each of our lives, none as much as Hunter's though, before she stood up and said,

"I have a pretty big day in the lab tomorrow, so I need

to get back to Little Rock. Thank you for taking the news as well as you did."

We each gave her a hug goodbye, wished her well, and walked her to the door. I was especially proud of myself for not shedding a single tear in Hunter's presence.

Once I was in bed that night though, the floodgates opened. I sobbed. For hours, I sobbed. Then once all my tears were dry, I thought to myself, *Why am I crying? She is happier than I've ever seen her. Am I crying for her, or am I crying for myself?* I knew the answer to my question, and I was ashamed of it. This was not a time to think of myself, I must focus on my family.

I spent the better part of the night talking with God. I begged Him to help me understand the process Hunter has been fighting every day of her life, and to please help me know how to help her in whatever way she will be needing help. I realized that all my sobbing had not been because of Hunter's news, but rather I was sobbing for me. For the fact that I will never see her walk down an aisle in a beautiful wedding dress, hold her newborn child to her breast as the baby nurses, or become the wonderful, amazing woman I've always known she will become, because now she will become the amazing, strong, man she feels she is destined to be.

In the month since Hunter told us of her plans to transform into a man, I think that Steve and I are handling the news better each day. At least I know that I am becoming more comfortable with the transformation, and I know that Steve is doing his best to accept the inevitable. As the saying goes, you can't put the genie back into the bottle. Even if we could put the genie back, I don't think we would want to after we see how truly happy Hunter is now.

Hunter began receiving the HRT, or testosterone injections a few months ago. I don't know who was more surprised at how quickly her voice dropped after she began the injections, us or her. She has mentioned to me that this change is occurring much more quickly than any of us had anticipated, including herself. I assured her that although there is a noticeable change in her voice register, she still sounds the same. She seemed relieved to hear that. I am just as relieved to discover that the Hunter I gave birth to is not going anywhere.

It's difficult to explain, but I see that her mannerisms are not changing at all, but her physical body will be undergoing the transformation. She was correct when she told me that she would always be the little girl in my memories. I still feel a sense of loss in some way that I can't justify. I don't know what it is a loss of... Possibly my dreams of grandchildren from Hunter? We have another daughter to fill that role if, and when, the time comes. I think it is a sadness for the difficult life Hunter has travelled thus far, the constant inner struggle within herself about her identity that she told us actually began 12 years ago.

When Hunter told us that she had been battling this from within for about 12 years, it broke my heart. It broke my heart, but not because I was disappointed in her revelation, but because I realized just how unhappy she must have been throughout those 12 years. I shed many tears just thinking of the confusion and inner turmoil she must have experienced. Tears will not help the situation as it now stands. I am pleased to be able to tell everyone that she is so much happier than I have ever seen her. She smiles a lot more frequently, laughs more, and seems so much more relaxed than she ever has been. Hunter *is* the same little girl from my memories. She is now and always will be, *and* she is going to change dramatically over the next few years during the transition process. I know that I will always love her, even when it becomes necessary to refer to her, as him.

I have spoken with both of my sisters and my parents about this several times, and they were as surprised as we were with Hunter's announcement, I feel as though Steve and I are forging into completely new territory. This trans world is new to us, and we are navigating this new terrain as best we can. I've been reading about it online and found there is a plethora of information available to us. There are many online support groups for parents of transgendered individuals, and just basic information that tells us it really isn't that rare.

In fact, in a report by the Williams Institute of UCLA, an estimated 3.5% of adults in the United States identify as lesbian, gay, and bisexual, with an estimated average of 0.3% identifying as transgender. This number, although dated, is actually a large number when you consider the population of the United States in July of 2015 was 321.488 million. My math skills are not my best facet, but I figured it comes to about 964,464 people in the United States who consider themselves transgender.

That is not a small number, and just as Multiple Sclerosis and Breast Cancer came to me without any prompting, this cause has found its way to me and I will proudly take up the cause of Transgender rights from this day forward. I will sign petitions, march in demonstrations, and do whatever I can as a mother of a transgender to help this group secure their rights as a definite part of our society. A society that is guaranteed certain unalienable rights in our constitution to live as productive members of our society. I cannot pray to God asking Him to protect my child from discrimination without stepping forward and putting my name firmly behind LGBT rights.

WORKS CITED

Gates, Gary J. "The Williams Institute." April 2011. *How many people are lesbian, gay, bisexual, and transgender?* <http://williamsinstitute.law.ucla.edu/wp-content/uploads/Gates-How-Many-People-LGBT-Apr-2011.pdf>.

"U.S. Census Bureau ." 11 October 2016. *Public Data.* <https://www.google.com/publicdata/explore?ds=kf7tgg1uo9ude_&hl=en&dl=en#!ctype=l&strail=false&bcs=d&nselm=h&met_y=population&scale_y=lin&ind_y=false&rdim=country&idim=country:US&ifdim=country&hl=en_US&dl=en&ind=false>.

Hunter and Sloan, 2015

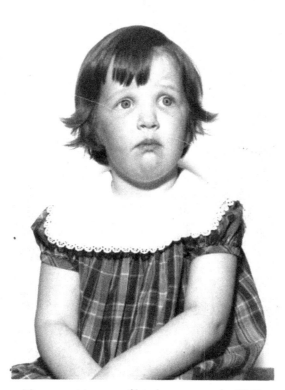

Nancy not in one of her better moods, 1965

Nancy Wasson Wayland, 2016

Hunter and Sloan 2014

Sloan and Hunter 2002

Nancy and Steve, 1991

The Wasson family, circa 1965

Printed in the United States
By Bookmasters